WOMEN'S MARCH ON THE PATH OF PROGRESS

(A Study of Decadal Change in Role Conflict)

WOMEN'S MARCH ON THE PATH OF PROGRESS

(A Study of Decadal Change in Role Conflict)

NILIMA SRIVASTAVA

SERIALS PUBLICATIONS
New Delhi (India)

First Published - 2005

ISBN: 81-86771-73-5

Published by

Head Office : **SERIALS PUBLICATIONS**
4, B.S.S. Hall, Khyber Pass Market
Civil Lines, Delhi-110054 (India)
Phone : 23245225
Fax : 91-11-23272135
E-mail: serials@satyam.net.in

Branch Office : 4830/24, Prahlad Street, Ansari Road
Darya Ganj, New Delhi-110002 (India)

PREFACE

With the change in status and role of women throughout the world, particularly after the organised movements started in west, there has been a lot of change in the status and role of women in India also, especially after Independence. The Constitution of India guaranteed equality of both the sexes in all walks of life. Today, women are not confined to the four-walls of their homes, but they perform variety of jobs in various fields. Despite the fact that women have started working outside, in our male dominated society, they are still required to perform domestic duties and shoulder responsibilities without much help from other members of the family. This multiplicity of roles, particularly in a situation in which it is difficult to make any decision regarding the relative significance of any one role, especially when both the roles are equally alluring, has led to a situation of conflicts. In such a situation the working women have to exercise their choice between the two incompatible but equally demanding roles. This conflicting situation has given rise to the problem of role conflict in working women. They face a Hobson's choice how to strike a balance between the two different type of roles, i.e. how to bring about a reconciliation between the conflicting demands of the two roles within a given frame of circumstances and working capacity which these women have. This is precisely the reason why it has been thought proper to conduct a study of role-conflict among working women professionals.

The study has been conducted on women professionals. Six professions have been chosen for this purpose. While choosing professions for the study, care has been taken to pick up not only women oriented professions, but also professions like law and engineering, where women are slowly but steadily carving their niche and others like medicine which is practised with ease by both men and women.

The professionally qualified women who have not been practising their professions have been left outside the purview of this study because it would have been difficult to find out such women in the universe and moreover the main purpose has been to study the role conflict created as a result of pursuit of professional practice.

The main objective of the study (1990) has been to study scientifically the various aspects of role-conflict among professionally qualified working women by exploring incidence, causes and effects, and to suggest measures for reducing the conflict. The nature of study has been diagnostic-cum-descriptive, and the effort has been mainly directed towards presenting a description of the various aspects of role conflict among working women professionals and also exploring the relationship between socio-economic background, type of family set up, type of atmosphere and culture at home domestic environment and such other variables on one hand and the role conflict on the other. The second study (2002) was undertaken with a view to assess the change that might have taken place as a result of change in societal preures for better standard of living.

Both the studies have been conducted within the corporation limits of Lucknow city by conducting detailed interviews. On the whole 272 professionals, 50 from each of the five professions of medicine, engineering, teaching, nursing and social work, were interviewed. Because of non availability of the required number (50) of lady lawyers only 22 female lawyers could be interviewed. In the study conducted in 2002, the size of the sample was restricted to 120 (20 from each profession).

Data required for the present study was collected by making use of the method of interview conducted with the help of a carefully constructed and pretested interview schedule. The collected data have been suitably edited, classified and tabulated, and logically as well as statistically analysed and interpreted, by collaborating the findings of the two studies.

The entire book has been divided into ten chapters. The chapters deal with introduction, theoretical framework of the study which include research design and methodology, profile of the respondents, incidence, reflectors, causes and effects of role conflict. The later chapters throw light on attitude and beliefs of the professionals, major findings and suggestions.

The crux of the findings of the present research is that being a part and parcel of largely traditional bound social system, professionally qualified working women, in addition to their best efforts to, effectively, perform their duties and responsibilities related to profession, also make their best efforts to carry out their family, house hold and social obligations, duties and responsibilities. With the passage of time there has been a change in the attitude of people towards working women and now they are more readily acceptable in the family and society at large. This is more true for professionally qualified women. But at times, due to child bearing and bringing up, stress and strain of the dual responsibilities is felt by the respondents.

In the 1990 study, largest percentage of professionals reported neither conflicting nor complementing situations when asked about the type of relationship between home and professional responsibilities. A larger number of them have reported complementary relationship then conflicting relationships in the present study.

Professionals in both the studies get help at home in taking up their domestic responsibilities. There is favourable attitude of their family torwards taking up of their profession and they are part of decision making mechanism in the family. For reducing role conflict among working women professionals respondents have also come out with various suggestions, both within and outside the home. The researcher has also made a few recommendations regarding the same.

ACKNOWLEDGEMENT

This voluminous and gigantic work could only be completed and sail through because of the providence of the Lord Almighty.

My Ph.D guide Prof Surendra Singh, presently the Vice Chancellor of Kashi Vidya Peeth, and then Head of Department, Social Work, Lucknow University provided his valuable guidance, unstinted encouragement, help and support in every manner possible. No words of gratitude can ever be expressed for the anchor he provided especially during the completion of my Ph.D. My profound devotion and deep respect for him, will never wither. I would like to remember all my teachers at my alma mater, Department of Social Work, Delhi University, where I am presently working, who at every stage of my studies from post- graduation onwards, have been deeply inspiring and guided me to scale greater heights. I will start with Prof R. M. Verma, who had sown the seeds of research by inducting me into his research team, soon after I finished my M.A. in 1981. Prof. Rajendra Singh has been instrumental in providing the much needed advice and encouragement from 1981. I pay him my sincere regards. My thanks are due to Prof. Aurna Bhardwaj and Prof. Sneh Lata Tandon for their strong and consistant support.

My sincere thanks are also due to my respondents in both the studies who gave their valuable time to have heart to heart talk with me. Quite a few of them showed great interest in knowing about the out come of the research.

I am grateful to the library staff of all the libraries which I consulted at various points of time. Sri Niketan Library, (Viswa Bharti University), Ratan Tata Library (Delhi School of Economics), Women Development Cell of Delhi University, Dr Zakir Hussain Library and Sarojini Naidu Centre of Women Studies (both Jamia Milia Islamia) and Departmental library of Social Work (DSSW). I would especially like to thank the staff of the library at DSSW, who untiringly kept locating various books which I consulted during the course of my second study.

On this occasion I would also like to thank Ms Alka Kumar who threw insight into the social work perspective to this work, by going through the draft of this script. I remember my other friends for their moral support.

I will be failing in my duty if I do not acknowledge my in-laws and parents, who have always appreciated and supported my efforts in my academic pursuits. Besides, my husband and daughter also need a mention for quietly bearing with me all the way. I had to complete this piece of work on time, and could not give them enough time when needed.

Lastly, my heart felt thanks are due to the publisher who showed his cooperation in bringing out this book in the shortest possible time.

NILIMA SRIVASTAVA

FOREWORD

Women in male-dominated Indian society have been discriminated against for thousands of years; and even today, despite the fact that they constitute about half of the population of our country and also that they have been guaranteed gender equality under the Constitution of India way back in 1950, are not enjoying status equal to that of men. Undoubtedly, a lot of changes have taken place in the position of women, particularly ,those who hail from upper castes or classes or who enjoy special privileges by virtue of their belonging to SCs, STs and OBCs. Women, by and large are not at the equal plane in different walks of life in our society. Social attitudes and values which prevail in Indian society even now are not conducive to proper growth and development of women. Moreover, they are considered either as an object of pleasure or as a chattel to be gifted away or sold. Even those women who are educated and gainfully employed are the victims of inequality in social relationships. Unfortunately, working women in India suffer from a double jeopardy on the one hand, as they lack in adequate approval for their participation in economically gainful work, on the other hand, they are required to bear and rear children and perform varied kinds of domestic chores. In such a scenario, women who muster enough courage to work outside suffer from role conflict which may broadly be defined as the tension resulting from mutually contradictory demands of the work place on the one hand, and households and other social obligations, on the other.

Women as a social category in Independent India have progressively advanced in the direction of development. Educationally, they have made great progress; economically, they have significantly advanced, and politically, they have actively participated in the political process, especially at the grass-root level in Panchayati Raj institutions and Urban Local Self-government because of 73rd and 74th Amendments in the Constitution. Because women today are much more empowered—educationally, economically and politically, the intensity of role conflict which they have been experiencing for pretty long time because of their participation in economically gainful outside work has also been considerably reduced. Dr. Nilima Srivastava who has obtained her Ph.D. Degree on the subject of Role Conflict among Women Professionals under my supervision way back in 1993 has further pursued her work by conducting another study on the same subject in the same locale in 2002 in order to find out whether any change has taken place in the gravity of role conflict experienced by the women in professions – like Medicine, Engineering, Teaching, Nursing, Law and Social Work. The first study has been based on 272 women professionals and the second one has incorporated within its ambit 120 women from these professions. She has collected bulk of invaluable data by conducting interview with the help of a well designed comprehensive interview schedule, and has compared the major trends emerging from both the studies after doing necessary processing of the collected data. Dr. Srivastava has presented her both the works in the form of the book entitled 'Women's March on the Path of Progress' which consists of 10 chapters beginning from Introduction and ending with Suggestions for Preventing and Minimizing Role Conflicts, with Theoretical Framework, Research Methodology, Profile of the Respondents, Incidence of Role Conflict, Causes of Role Conflict, Effects of Role Conflict, Attitudes and Beliefs of the professionals, and Major Findings and Conclusions in between. Her conclusions are highly revealing; and suggestions are extremely useful.

The book on the whole provides great insight into the change that has taken place in the area of role conflict experienced by women in professions and establishes that women professionals in India have been continuously marching on the path of progress because of availability of varied kinds of opportunities to them in diverse areas of education, economically gainful work and politics in the Independent India.

I am sure that the book will be of immense use to all those who are interested in women's issues and who want to promote gender equality in all spheres of life and living in India in order that the dream of democracy as a way of life in this country may be truly realized.

(PROF.) SURENDRA SINGH

Vice-Chancellor
Mahatma Gandhi
Kashi Vidyapeeth
Varanasi

Varanasi
Maha Shivaratri,
The 18th February,
2004

CONTENTS

CHAPTER 1

INTRODUCATION

There was a time when men exclusively worked outside home and women looked after the household affairs, confining themselves to the four walls of their home. But times have changed. Today, the modern social conditions have made a powerful impact on the role of women. They have emerged out of their household cocoons.

The scenario of the modern society has changed. In the past, women were assigned only feminine role, like cooking, cleaning, sweeping, looking after children and other gender specific work, consisting of household chores and related duties. The men with rugged bodies, were given roles outside the house . They used to be the bread-earner for the family, taking care of the economic responsibilities. Thus the entire family's work was divided into two units with separate responsibilities for males and females. Both the members performed their assigned duties within the framework of family. The working of the family, thus, went on smoothly.

Function of the primary unit of family done by

Male → Outside work

Female → Inside work

The pattern of society has undergone a change because of the change in prevailing economic, social and political situations in the country. The process of change has been quite rapid in India. In the post Independence period, people in general had to face various challenges. There came a swift change in the thinking pattern of the society with regard to women, especially in the sphere of education, followed by her stepping out as a working women. Women have accepted new roles by moving outside their narrow world of household chores to fulfil their needs and aspirations. *Neera Desai (1957 : 247) has remarked : The modern woman is slowly breaking through the shell of a narrow domestic existence and is beginning to participate in the larger life of the nation and even humanity*[1].

Every changed step of life and society leads to a different set of problems and conflicts. Eversince women were confronted with this bitter truth, they stood at the threshold of a new era of changed values, where they had to work in a male dominated atmosphere without much respite from their duties and responsibilities at home.

Therefore, the old and the new roles, traditional and the professional responsibilities, values and norms put the working women in a situation rife with conflict and tension.

Historical perspective of the status of women in India

The status of women in Hindu society has undergone change from time to time. Their position in it has been variedly estimated and diametrically opposite views prevail, regarding their place in different stages of civilization.

Women in vedic times enjoyed a very high status. They enjoyed atmost equal rights as men at that time. Women in field of intellect were men's equal. They composed and chanted vedic hymns at the holy sacrifices. They had the fullest freedom of thought and action; Ghosa, Godha, Agastya-svaha, Aditi, Indrani, Sachi, Urvasi, Lopa Mudra, Yarni *et al* were renowned scholars of vedic period.

The Upnishad form the latter philosophic part of the vast vedic literature, and here we find two glorious names of Maitreyi and Gargi.

Thus, Vedic women were not-only chronologically but also educationally, socially, culturally; and they will forever stand before the whole world as eternal emblems of Jnana-Bhakti-Karma, also Satya-Siva-Sundara to the lasting benefit of all women, all over the world, all through out the ages.[2] (Renuka Ray 1978, p.18).

But the literature also throws light on the other aspect of the status of women of that era. The later tenets generally enjoins that the males are the masters of women and set the conclusion thus: their father protect them in their childhood; their husband protect them in their youth, and their sons protect them in their old age. A woman is never considered fit to be independent.

On the one hand, she is considered little more than a slave or beast of burden, bonded to drudgery, bought as a cattle and treated as such. On the other hand those who have had anything to do with tribes reckoning descent from the mother are likely to view a women as the undisputed mistress of the family, if not of community life.

It appears to me, remarks Tara Ali Baig, that Vedic women were probably comparable to modern Indian women–the upper strata or the very gifted one, permitted every advantage of education, with the capacity to rise to the highest status and authority, while injustice and impediments hamper the life of the women at lower ends.[3] (Devendra Kiran, 1985 p. xiii).

During the epic age also, the status of women was high. Women, in matters of selecting their partners in marriage, had equal rights. The marriage of Sita and Droupadi were conducted through Swayamvara.

Prepuberty marriages were unknown. A woman who had the capacity to choose a husband must have been probably a grown up one.

Widow remarriages were in existence. If the husband died, the wife could marry again by performing Aja-Panchoudana–sacrifice in the memory of a deceased husband. Women had the privilage of adoption as well. This was the status of women in vedic period, and during the age of the great epics.

In the Sutra period the position of woman was not so high as that in the vedic times. The Aryans who had migrated to India were merely a handful. Hence their man-power was wasted away in their fights against aborigines of India. It was the spirit of time to crave for more male children, because they wanted more men to fight against aborigines. Males of all ranks were looked upon with preferential treatment. Women were relegated to house-hold duties. Hence the shadow of the ill-treatment of non-Aryan women casts its evil seeds upon the dignity of Aryan women. Polygamy naturally entered into the social life of Aryans. The Aryans were using 'Soma'-a mild and a useful beverage in the colder region and a stronger drink "Sura". Women were gradually proved to be incapable of using these intoxicating drinks, which went round men and women at the time of performing sacrifices. As the drinks were served at the vedic sacrifices, women in course of time were left out as they were not using the drinks. As women did not participate in the sacrificial ceremonies, they eventually began to lose touch with the vedas and finally the study of the vedas fell into the hands of men who monopolised their study.

As the study of vedas, the only source of knowledge became the monopoly of man, women were pushed back to domestic duties. Day by day the gulf between man and woman widened. As a result of this, women's right to enjoy equal status with man deteriorated.

Badarayana and Jaimini fought at this time for the revival of womanhood on vedic injunctions. They pleaded for equal rights of woman. But the time were against them. Woman had already been kept out of vedic sacrifices and from the study of vedas. The culture of the Aryans was in part assimilated with the culture of the Dasyus. These circumstances led to the degradation of Aryan womanhood. They were deprived of all the rights to property, inheritance and adoption. Men regarded women as property. So women were classed among the land, cattle and other kind of temporal wealth.

Vasistha and Bandhayana were also hard on women. They said that men were their masters and so women should never be independent. Since women were regarded as property, marriage by purchase came into existence. Widows were ordained to lead a strict ascetic life.

It seems that at the end of this period a revival of womanhood had taken place. The wife had gained equal rights to property with her husband. Yet the widow was not allowed to inherit the property.

In medieval times, Padmini the heroine, Ahalyabai the great administrator, enlightened the people with their scholarship. Lakshmi devi wrote. "Vivida Chandra". This period is also known for the works of the great authoress Kalyani, sister of Madhvacharya. Women in this period enjoyed quite a high status.

The 18th century, perhaps was the darkest period so far as the Indian women were concerned. Political decay following the disruption of the Mughal Empire and disorder due to the advent of various European powers came hard on women.

The 18th century with its "intellectual stagnation" manifested in decay of knowledge and learning, completed with social degeneration, worsened the conditions of Indian women.

Again the foreign invasion brought deterioration in the position of women. Muslim conquerors imposed their coersive and rigid norms on the Hindu society, curtailing the rights, freedom and status of women.

Polygamy among the wealthier section and the 'kulins, early marriage, sati rites, killing of female child etc. became rampant. This was combined with fossilized customs, tradition, superstitions and irrational bigotry[4] (Basu, 1978 : 36).

Later during the Moughal period, the Moughal Emperors introduced certain reforms trying to relieve the hardship of women. Akbar, the great, allowed a definite share in property in his effforts to improve the deteriorating conditions of women. But the efforts were next to negligible.

In the beginning of British Administration in India, the position of women further deteriorated. It was declared that the Indians should be ruled by their own law with regards to succession, inheritance, marriage alliances and religion. They adopted "the non-intervention policy". The English people translated Manu's code at first and brought it into practice. This law pinned the pepetual tutelage of the women. Women went back imperceptibly in social status. The advancement of the British rule robbed women of their rights to enjoy equal status with men.

Awakening of Women

After complete deterioration in the position of women, slowly she regained her position and status. In 1880 some reforms took place to improve the status of women. In the history of Indian Women's struggle for liberty from all social bondages and right of equality, perhaps the most eventfully period was the 19th century, that saw the dawn of new Indian women with liberalization as their basic principle.

Raja Ram Mohan Roy and Bipin Chandra Pal were the pioneers of this era who gave impetus to the process of emancipation of women by fighting against derogatory customs of the society against women. Barely after half a century, it was unimaginable, that exhilarating, exalting changes and reforms or improvements would have ever been brought in all spheres of women's lives and activities, without any violent feminist movement of the suffragist type, as found in European countries. Owing to the spread of English education and the inter-mixing of western and eastern cultures, the women of India began to realise their importance in society and organised themselves to regain their original status.

The various socio-religious organisations, such as Arya Samaj, Brahma Samaj etc. gave a great impetus to the awakening of Indian womanhood. Educated women came forward demanding equal rights with men. Ramabai Ranade, Sarala Devi, Chowda Rani, Saroj Nalini and a host of others are known for their valuable service for uplifting the position of women. Women organisations were formed and as a result of the services of these women organisations, the status of women improved. The women leaders further found warm sympathisers and active supporters among men also. The main programmes of these organisations were to educate women, to abolish systems like purdah and child marriages and to improve the lot of widows.

Change in scene

The women of India received a political impetus in 1930, when the Indian National Congress launched the Civil Disobedience Movement. This movement was like a swift lightening process. The chains of restraint fell silently from the wrists of women which had fettered them so long. Ancient prejudices vanished; walls of traditions cracked, and the ray of new hopes crept into their mind with a dream of a better and free world. The status accorded to women was as a result of the intense fight of the women's organization. Under the able guidance of Sarojini Naidu, Vijayalakshmi Pandit, Kasturba Gandhi, Raj Kumari Amrit Kaur, Kamla

Devi Chattopadhyaya and Mahatma Gandhi, the women's organization strengthened.

Guru Rabindra Nath Tagore said in his address in 1931 to the Annual Session of the All India Women's conference which met in Calcutta that year: *"The cadence of human civilization is disjointed and the harmony can only be restored, when man and woman contribute in equal measure. This can not happen by woman becoming duplicates and imitators of man. It is for them to strike a new line, a new note through which the mistakes and failures of today are circumcised and overcome"*[5] *(Ray, 1978 : 7).*

Educational amenities revolutionized the status of women, Gandhiji (1958: 134) wrote that *"(Education) develops and sharpens one's intellect and it increases one's capacity of doing".*[6] Women tried to examine the old orthodox views of Hinduism and tried to assert their equal status with men. This awakening of thought in Indian women led to their increased participation in public activities and broke down the traditional conceptions and loosened the social bounding in which they were held for a long time.

Increasing contact with western liberalization, growing social consciousness and formation of numerous reform societies led to the awakening of the masses also.

Swami Vivekanand advocated that Indian women should be emancipated from their social bondage. About education, he said that, ideal education should be one, which should best enable every woman in time, to come, to resume into herself the greatness of all the women of the Indian past[7] *(Basu , 1978 : 48).*

It might be observed that whatever transformation in the human community has resulted out of developments in technology, means of communication, growth in industry, political consciousness, and morality is reflected in social attitudes, social relations, organizations, control and opportunity. This also affected the oriental outlook, modes of life, attitudes, desires and ambition of women. Women shed the seclusion of their homes and took their place side by side with men in almost all walks of life.

The suffragist movement and winning of equal political rights with those enjoyed by men lifted women out of their traditional status of seclusion, dependence and inferiority. A new consciousness of freedom and equality manifested itself in such details as dress, association, occupation, marriage, house holding, recreation, sports, travel and business.

The two great world wars were no small stimuli to drag women out of seclusion of their homes for occupations which demanded alertness of mind and body. The great significant contribution of the war-years is the admission of the middle class and respectable sections of the women of the community to the acceptance of the tasks that a generation ago would have been considered intruding. The old classification of job as exclusively men's and equally exclusively women's, failed.

Women in Independent India

The war-years revealed that there was scarcely a job that a man could do, which a woman could not. In a machine-age which, to a large extent eliminated the necessity to employ naked brute strength or muscle power, there are almost no job which can be exclusive to men.

The development of several women's organizations, legislations regarding marriage, remarriage, divorce, property rights of women, regulations of wages, maternity benefits, crèches, higher jobs and growth of education among women, reservation for women and changing social conditions revolutionized the social status of women in post independence era. All these made the social climate conducive for women to step out and work for the country and society at large.

The first two five years plans referred to the problems of women's education and sought to link higher professional education and occupation. The Report of the Committee on the Education of Women in 1959 further substainted the efforts. Later the National Education Policy, 1986 and The National Perspective Plan (1988-2000) also shed light on educating and empowering women and reducing inequality and disparity.

Promilla Kapur (1975 : 42) remarks: *The urban educated middle and upper class working women comprise comparatively a recent emerging social group which is drawing the attention of laymen as well as the scholars. Its emergence in itself is an indication of the significant socio-economic and politico-legal changes taking place in our country*[8].

The UN Commission on the status of women and specialized agencies of the UN have taken initiative from time to time to throw light on this subject and have framed resolutions to its effects. Education and gender equality are at the centre stage of contemporary discourse on development.

More recently gender has been identified as a crucial category which divides people and which in addition to race, ethnicity, class and caste, deserves attention in the education equality paradigm[9]. *(Channa, 2000 : 1012)*

The profound social changes that India has witnessed in the last 50-60 years or so have affected its entire population. Yet in some sections of the society their impact has been much more marked than in others.

Among the middle class urban educated population, these changes have affected woman much more than man. The changed socio-economic conditions, particularly after Independence, have widened especial opportunities for women's education, leading to new openings of employment and other avenues of professional growth. This has provided them with new spheres to express and assert their equality.

But much remains to be done before a woman is able to attain that status in society through which she could play an effective role and her special contribution of some consequence.

Family responsibilities Vs. Professional responsibilities

When a woman takes up a profession she has a dual status and a dual role to play. She has to shoulder two very different types of responsibilities. She works like a male professional at the work-place and cannot shy away from her responsibilities and duties at home which she has to perform like any non-working woman. She tries to perform at the highest level of efficiency on both fronts. To survive in the male dominated atmosphere and because of stiff competition she has to be alert and efficient at the place of work. But if she neglects her duties at home she suffers from a guilt which can even affect her professional outlook.

Genesis of Role - Conflict

To speak of the conflicts arising out of women performing double role in the home and at place of work makes sense only on the backdrop of this patriarchal-bourgeois concept of society according to which woman is defined by her biological functions. This is more true of middle class women. Lower class–agricultural labours, road construction labour, factory worker, scavengers or maid, do not have problems of role conflict. They are free from the demand of the role norms of the 'decent' middle class woman.

The woman who has adopted the profession may be doing it for many reasons, viz. to add to the income of the family, to better use her professional talent or may be having any other specific objective in mind. But, she never forgets her primary role as well in the family with which she is very closely associated. When she is not able to discharge these duties, she suffers from guilt. She wants to upgrade her social status and satisfy her professional instinct by taking up the profession but she is caught by the role conflict. *Pratima Bhatiya (1976 : 07) has stated her views in these words: "They are confronted with a situation when they have already opted for a job and entered a new role of a modern woman. This is the genesis of the problem when tradition is not being wholly abandoned and the modern is not being fully adopted.*[10]

With the two contradictory roles which demand her time and energy, often put her in conflicts. Kapoor (1975 : 19) has opined; *"Now she has two roles to perform, one of a house wife and the other of a wage earner. Both these roles make demand on her time and energy. She is quite often torn between the conflicting pulls of the dual role.*[11]

The outer reality characterized by conflict in roles create inner conflict in mind. This gets reflected overtly in many forms and creates conflicting social situations, thus further aggravating the intensity of conflict. Gerland R Grace (1972 : 01) has explained the cause of conflict in the following manner: *Role-Conflict, role-strain or role-stress are all concerned with problems for the individual which arise as the result of incapability.*[12] Among the Indian women, role conflict arise out of the problems of differences in the expectations of the individuals. A working women is emotionally, intectually more evolved and socially more aware of her rights and privileges. This infact increase the level of role conflict.

Gandhiji (1958 : 178) had also pointed out; *the awakening of civil and political consciousness among Indian women has created a conflict between the traditional domestic duties and the duty towards the society.*[13] A state of confusion is created because of the contradictory nature of the dual role. Kapoor (1979 :19) has rightly observed, *"In the transitional era there is a role-confusion because of the absence of fitness between her roles as a worker and as a house-wife and mother also because of the tension that is created due to her inner conflict.*[14]

A married woman has to do all the household chores as a house-wife. But she also wants to come out of her house to share the economic burden of the family. Myrdal Klein (1970 : 07) has been of the view; *If women now makes an articulate and conscious effort to go out in the world, they are not driven by a sudden wave of perversity or fashion, but by the simple logic of economics.*[15]

If the problem of role conflict is reviewed in the context of classes in the society, it will come to light that it is a typically middle class urban problem where fortunately girls get an opportunity to receive good and high education of their choice and aptitude, and develop consciousness of male-female equality. But when they get married and look for job satisfaction with settled married life partner, they start feeling the stress and strain of extra burden of working outside, in addition to discharge of their normal family responsibilities. And it is here that the problem of role conflict arises.

But the scene is slowly changing and working women are being accepted by the family and the society at large. As a result of urbanization, industrialization and modernization, globally more and more women are coming out and taking up varied kind of professions which were unheard of, even in the recent past.

The middle class women take greater interest to do lucarative jobs to cope with the emerging economic compulsions. Now the men are opting for working women through marriage for having supplementry regular income for the family.

Reddy (1986 : 15) referred to the excerpt by Kapadia, who says, *"Another factor of importance affecting the family is the employment of women, which has become possible through education and present economic strains. Today, even the members of the older genreation desire that the educated daughter-in-low must help the family by supplementing its income. Not only those women who are economically hard-pressed get engaged in remunerative jobs, but also those who wish to live a socially useful life and not to subsist on the family income. They have come to realise that work gives them personal status and indepedent-social standing"*[16].

Slowly and slowly the roles are becoming less defined and mellowing for the working women, especially at the home front and competition on the professional front takes her mite now. And with better understanding of the problems of the working women by the society in general and more pragmatic approach on the part of the professional, the gap of expectations and non-fulfilment can be reduced, thereby reducing the conflict, stress or tension involved.

References

1. Desai, Neera : Women in Modern India, Vora and Company, Bombay, 1957, p. 247.

2. Ray, Renuka (Ed.) : Role and Status of Women in Indian Society, FIRMA, KLM Pvt. Ltd, Calcutta ,1978: p. 18.

3. Devendra, Kiran : Status and Position of Women in India, Vikas Publishing House, Ghaziabad, 1985 p. XIII.

4. Basu, Krishna : Role and Status of Women in Indian Society, FIRMA, KLM Pvt. Ltd., Calcutta , 1978: p 36.

5. Ray, Renuka (Ed) : Role and Status of Women in Indian Society, FIRMA, KLM Pvt. Ltd., Calcutta, 1978: p 7.

6. Gandhi, M.K. : Women and Social Injustices; Navjeewan Publishing House, Ahemdabad, 1958, p. 134.

7. Basu, Krishna : Role and Status of Women in Indian Society, FIRMA, KLM Pvt. Ltd., Calcutta, 1978: p 48.

8. Kapoor, Promila : The Changing Status of Working Women; Vikas Publishing House Pvt. Ltd., New Delhi 1979, p.42.

9. Channa, Karuna : Treading the Hollowed Halls, Economic and Political Weekly, March 8, 2000 p. 1012.

10. Bhatia, Pratima : Role Conflict Among Working Women: Unpublished Thesis of Lucknow University, 1976, p.07.

11. Kapoor, Promilla : The Changing Status of Working women, Vikas Publishing House Pvt. Ltd., New Delhi 1979, p.19.

12. Gerald, R. Grace : Role Conflict and the Teacher, Routledge and Kegan Paul, London, 1972, p. 01.

13. Gandhi, M.K. : Women and Social Injustice; Navjeewan Publishing House, Ahemdabad, 1958, p.178.

14. Kapoor, Promila: The Changing Status of Working Women; Vikas Publishing House Pvt. Ltd., New Delhi 1979, p. 07.

15. Myrdal, Alva and Villa, Klein : Women's Two Roles Home and Work; Rautledge and Kegan Paul Ltd., London, 1970, p.07.

16. Reddy, C.R : Changing Status of Educated Working Women, B.R. Publishing Corporation, Delhi, 1986, p. 15.

CHAPTER 2

THEORETICAL FRAMEWORK REASARCH DESIGN AND METHODOLGY

Every society has a scheme of stratification by which it divides itself into permanent groups or categories linked to each other by a feeling of superiority or subordination. All groups are inter-related to each other as per the scheme of stratification, and have different place or positions inter-linked to each other in such a way that varied kinds of needs of their individual members are met satisfactorily. These positions are embedded, or carry with them varied kinds of rights on the one hand, and duties and responsibilities on the other, widely recognised by members of the group per se, as also by member of various other inter-related groups in the society.

Concept of Status

The rank or a place or position of the individual occupying it, in the prestige-hierarchy of the group and community at large, in terms of various rights associated with it, is its sociological status.

Most sociologists define status as a postion occupied by an individual in a social system[1] *(Blackwell Dictionary of Sociology 2000 : 309).*

Status is purely a relational term which means that each status exists only through its relation to one or more other statuses, for example, husband and wife. Wife has no status without a husband and vice-verse. The status may be manifested or dormant.

In many groups, an individual has many statuses. Not only that, even in any one single group itself, a person holds more than one status. This multiplicity of statuses is sociologically designated as status-set.

The sum total of the statuses that we occupy is known as a status-set. The status-set locates an individual in relation to the multidimentional network of social system that make up the system we live in.

Every sociological position carries with it not only rights enjoyed by its occupants but also enjoins upon the incumbent to discharge varied kinds of duties and responsibilities. As the rights and duties are inter-dependent in nature, in as much as they reinforce each other, rights cannot be thought of in the absence of duties. These are always contibutary & complementary to each other. It is therefore implied that every status having certain given rights also enjoins upon its occupant to carry out and discharge certain duties and responsibilities. The activites which the incumbent of a particular position enjoying a certain status performs or the part that he or she plays, is referred to as role, in sociology.

Concept of *Role*

Blackwell Dictionary of Sociolgoy (2000 : 263) defines role as a set of ideas associated with a social status that define its relationship with another position in a social system.[2]

In society, the status of a person determines the kind of role he or she plays. According to Merill Elliot (1976; 09). *"Role is the part played as a result of each status". Status is defined as the position which the individual occupies in the group by virtue of one's sex, age, family, occupation, marriage and achievement.*[3]

The term r*ole* has been borrowed from stage. Later on social scientists related this term to the real life, when we presume or expect some special type of behaviour from the individual acquiring different types of *status* in social structure. This world is a stage where every individual has to play certain "set of roles" in society. In social sciences' terminology, *role* is an important term because it affects the social system and structure of a society. In real life an individual has to play different set of roles according to the status acquired or assigned to him or her. In fact, *roles* are the set of expected functions or behaviour required of an individual to perform.

Lexicon Universal Encyclopaedia (Vol. 16: 271) describes role *as the set of expectations associated with a person's position in a social organisation. For every status there is an associated role, a set of expectations about behaviour.*[4]

Any role is guided by beliefs, values and attitude of people who play the role and also those among whom the role is played.

Penguin Dictionary of Psychology (1986 : 650) defines role as : *It refers generally to any pattern of behaviour involing certain rights, obligations and duties which an individual is expected to be trained and indeed, encouraged to perform in a given social situation.*[5]

The Dictionary of Family Psychology and Family Therapy (1993 : 343) describe role as *the expected behaviour of the family members.*[6]

Roles can be ascribed or achieved. Ascribed roles are assigned on the factors on which the individual has no control, for example gender, race, etc. While the achieved roles are earned on the basis of individual achievements–becoming a boss, bread winner or a scape goat. The two kinds of roles may overlap in the family.

Since a person enjoys different statuses, he or she performs different roles also. There are three aspects of role: (i) Expectations which other members of a group or various groups in society pin on the incumbent referred to as **role expectation.** (ii) What the incumbent actually does in course of discharge of varied kinds of duties and responsibilities, expected of him or her is called **role-performance,** and (iii) What a group or various groups in society prescribe for the incumbent of a particular position having a particular status is termed as **role-prescription**.

Every institution or organisation determines the role of its constituent units. Each unit has to perform the required and expected role in order to maintain the functioning of the institution. The family is the fundamental institution of society. The units of the family are mother, father and children. Each unit has to perform some specific type of work according to the established social norms. In general, father earns the money and is a breadwinner. While mother is the chief care provider talking, playing and caring for each other, are some bonds through which they are bound. She is, infact a mover and shaker of each unit in the family and as such her role is pivotal. It is necessary to maintain the links within a family for its proper functioning as an institution.

As a person's behaviour is largely determined by the role he or she is performing at any given time, each person has to perform different roles in a complex society. In a simple society, the roles are simple in nature and have no tussle between them. As the complexity of the society increases the role tussles also increases.

Role conflict

An incumbent of a particular position having a particular status, has to deal with different categories of people in the group, of which he is a member. In course of his or her dealings with them, he or she perform different types of roles, each with a set of its own duties. These different types of roles are referred to as role-set. Apart from this, the incumbent of a position having a particular status has other statuses also which enjoins upon him or her to perform various types of duties and responsibilities, termed as role-multiplicity. And it is here, in the context of role-set and role-multiplicity, arises another concept, called or known as **role-conflict**.

Role conflict according to the Dictionary of Family Psychology (1993 . 340) is a conflict arising from disparities between family members, perception of each others roles.[7] Each family member also has a concept of the roles of the other members. However, one's conception of one's own role and the conception of other member of that role may differ.

Along with the concept of status and role, role conflict plays an important part in drawing attention to the connection between individual experience and behaviour, and the cultural and structural characteristics of social system from which the potential for conflict and strain emerges.

According to the Penguin Dictionary of Sociology (1986:182), *role conflict is used in various senses. (i) When a person finds he or she is playing two or more roles at one time that make incompatible demands, as often happens, for example with those working women who have to satisfy simultaneously the role expectations as a professional, a wife and a mother, which may give rise to conflicting demands. (ii) When a person defines his or her role in one way while those in related roles define it differently, as may happen when a teacher adheres to his or her own code of professional behaviour which are disputed by parents or local education authorities. (iii) When related roles have incompatible expectations of the focal role, as in the case of a foreman subjected to conflicting expectations from workers and manager*[8].

Role conflict, according to Blackwell Dictionary of Sociology (2000 : 264) occurs when people are confronted with contarary or incompatible role expectation in various social status they occupy in lives.[9]

Role-conflict takes several different forms. When conflicts involves roles associated with two different statuses such as employee and a parent, the result is called **status-strain**. When the conflicting roles are both associated with the same status say a military ofiicer rendered to send his troops on a risky operation. It is known as **role-strain**. Conflicts may occur when people disagree about what the expectations are for a particular role. In another sense, role conflict can occur when some one simply has difficulity in satisfing the expectations because their duties are unclear, too difficult or disagreeable.

The Penguin Dictionary of Psychology (1986:651) conceptualises *role conflict as a situation, in which a person is expected to perform two or more roles that are in conflict, in fundamental ways with each other*[10]. *In the opinion of Krech, Crutchfield and Ballachey (1962:530), role conflict refers to "the situation" in which an individual is expected to play two roles that involve responses that are competing or antagonistic*[11]. *Explaining role conflict in terms of conflict of norms in total behaviour of an individual,* Nadel (1969: 65) describes it as *a conflict between the roles he is to made assume*[12].

In the light of these views, the term role conflict may be defined as "incompatibility between different types of roles performed as a part of role-set or role-multiplicity". It refers to a situation in which the incumbent of a particular status is required to play two or more roles that involve duties and responsibilities making competing or antagonistic demands.

In this study, role conflict is taken as created only due to role playing. This is responsible for role tension and disturbance in the mind, due to the inability to live up to other people's expectations. *Ralph (1976:10) has rightly observed, Where the roles cannot be kept separate, the conflict is likely to cause discomfort. This can happen when one is required to play two roles at the same time*[13].

According to *Sutherland and L. Robert (1966:77), role conflicts are the contradictory role behaviour expected of persons in the same position.*[14] In the opinion of Ralf (1976:08), it may also arise when different people expect a role to be played in different ways.

Thus, it can be concluded that role conflict takes place in two situations. Firstly, when the contradictory role is expected to be played by a single person, and secondly, when different people expect role to be played in different ways by a person. In this study, the working woman is generally expected to play two types of contradictory roles, the role of a traditional women, and the role of a modern professional.

Role conflict among working women professionals in the Indian context

Indian society is in a stage of transition in which our traditional social set up is being gradually replaced by a modern one. This process of transformation has affected all sections of our society, irrespective of their sex, age, religion, caste and class. Women, in terms of their status and role are also experiencing this change. Traditionally, women in India were required to perform duties and responsibilities related to household work alone. But today, because of varied kind of external as well as internal factors and forces, arising from the market of western materialism, women are compelled by the exigencies of situation, in which they are placed, to take up work outside the four walls of the house. In this regard, Neera Desai (1957:247) writes: *The modern woman is slowly breaking through the shell of a narrow domestic existence and is beginning to participate in the large life of the nation and even humanity*[15]. Wadley (1977: 91) has remarked that *urbanisation, industrialisation and modernization are the chief forces which drove our women into work force*[16].

Today, a woman who has attained a particular qualification in a specialised profession and is desirous of practising it with zeal and enthusiasm is caught in a conflicting situation mainly because she is a mother/daughter-in-law/ wife/sister at home with which are associated certain duties and responsibilities. Both the roles are equally attractive and demanding and create a situation of conflict and cause strain for the incumbent.

Chakraborty (1978 : 16) argues that *while many middle class women with a university education prefer to marry and perform their usual roles as wives and mothers, they also concurrently prefer to seek employment opportunities so that their educational training can be used to enhance family's living standard*[17]

However, different people expect these roles to be performed differently. Different roles played by professionally qualified women in different spheres, is diagrammatically presented in fig.2.1

A woman has no problem in playing the traditional role till she is in her home turf. A woman is bound to play all these feminine roles because of her ascribed status. The other roles she plays are due to her achieved status. Both of these statuses are entirely different in nature and so are the role patterns.

Fig : 2.1 : Places and Types of Roles Performed by the Professionals.

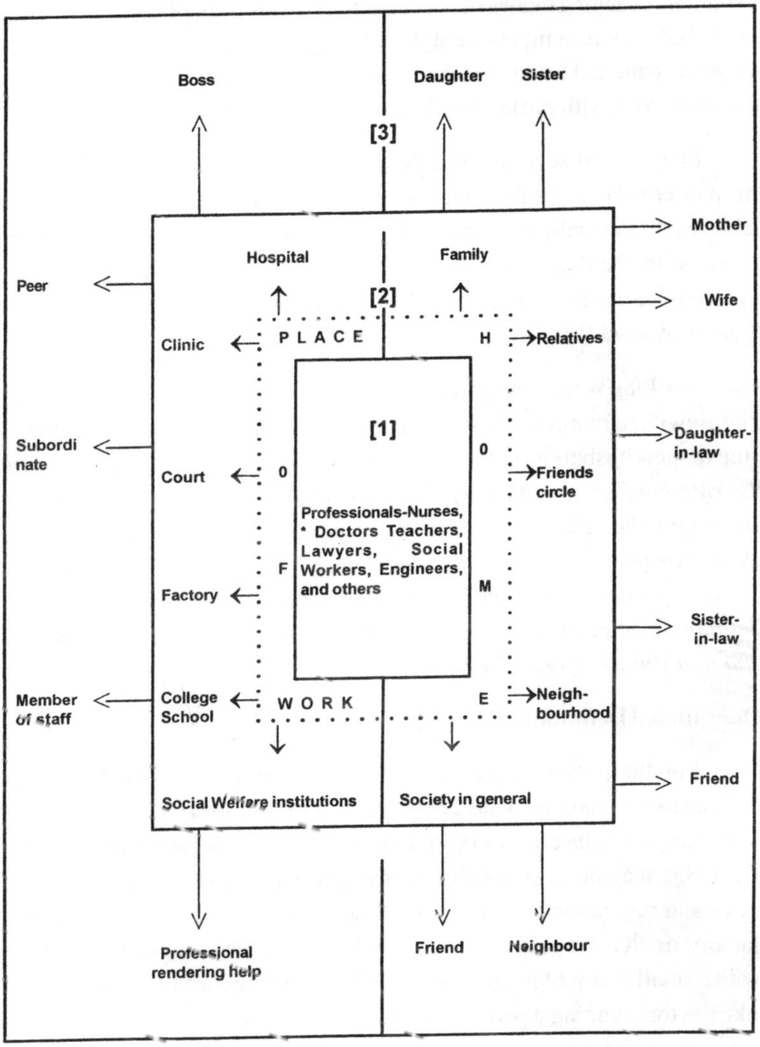

[1]. Type of Professionals.

[2]. Places where she has to perform different roles.

[3]. Different types of roles which she has to perform.

Social changes directly influence the role patterns. Industrial revolution, changing modes of production, evolving technologies, increased level of education, competitive style of living have all altered the traditional set family pattern. Her age old work at home (feminine work) is now tagged upon her along with professional work (occupational work).

Playing two sets of roles, the traditional gender specific one, and the modern day's professional one, is easier aimed, aspired for, and achieved than actually performed. At times, working women find it difficult to adjust to the dual roles. Reddy (1986: 101) has remarked, *they are unable to adjust to the dual roles and are strained and compelled by the burden of work*[18].

Working women may not be able to properly perform their roles of a housewife, a mother, a host etc. They may not be able to give sufficient time to their husbands, to their children, the in-laws, guests or friends. *In the role conflict to which the Indian woman is exposed to due to her entry into the relatively new sphere of professional activity, may be termed as inter-role conflicts. These inter-role conflicts are caused by the acceptance of two or more roles, directed by their own set of definitions by each set of expectations, and which cannot be avoided.*[19] *Jha and Pujari (1996 : 149)*

Operational Definition

For the present study, a working woman professional has been defined as a woman who has completed her professional qualification for a specialized nature of work and is also pursuing a career in the same field. She may be employed in an institution where she is guided by the rules and regulations of the administration, like engineers working in a factory or she is a self-employed professional, who single handedly or with a small group of people carries on with the practice of the profession like doctors running a private clinic.

Those women who are professionally qualified but have not taken up any job have been left out of the purview of the present study because, first it will be difficult to trace out such women in the universe and second, the present study aims at studying the role conflict arising out of pursuing a career.

To streamline the research, respondents from only six professions have been studied, mainly because most of the women opt for these socially prestigious and financially secured professions. The other aim has been to select professions where varied kind of situations can be studied, for instance long working hours, changing duty timing, challenging male dominated jobs and relatively easy going and female oriented jobs.

Lastly the study had to be conducted within the corporate limits of Lucknow City and these female professionals could be approached without much difficultly.

The six categories of professionals are:

(1) Medical Doctors (2) Lawyers

(3) Engineers (4) Teachers

(5) Nurses (6) Social Workers

The Universe

The Universe of the two studies has been constituted by women who are professionally qualified for six specialized professions. These women are making use of their professional expertise either in a formal organization (employed) or pursuing their profession on their own (private practice). In either case these women professionals are practising their profession and making use of their professional knowledge.

Both the studies have been conducted with in the corporation limits of the city of Lucknow, the capital of Uttar Pradesh State.

Many research studies have been undertaken to probe into the role conflict and its related aspects, which arise out of multiple roles played by working women.

This is a study which specifically deals with role conflict arising out of shouldering two types of responsibilities in the backdrop of the fact that the women have attained specialized professional education and training for the practice of the profession. The compartive study focuses on the change in pattern and incidences of role conflict after a span of 12 years, when the new set of societal norms and expections are prevalent.

Moreover the culture of a place and the pravailing environment also play an important role in determining such aspects, more so for the females.

Results would have been different for a small town study, a metropolitan city and a place falling in between these two extremes of urban living.

Methodology

The method adopted for eliciting the responses was that of interview – the reason for choosing this method was that it is a means of establishing communication with the respondents including spoken words, gestures and expressions. Interview being a two way communication, for a meaningful exchange of views covering both objective and subjective elements, becomes an important tool for a face to face contact, with accompanying interaction and inter stimulation.

While conducting the interview with the help of an interview schedule the following techniques were employed

1. Introduction

a. Explaining the purpose and objectives of the research

b. Describing the method by which the respondent was selected

c. Stating the confidential nature of the interview

2. Standardization of interview

Interview schedule contained mostly close-ended questions, providing the possible options to the respondents to choose the one matching their choice. In case the response was not amongst the options, it was also recorded separately.

3. Stimulating the complete responses

To get the complete response on different issues, questions were explained by giving examples in general.

4. Recording the responses

This was done with utmost accuracy and responses which were not directly related to the question but were helpful in formalizing the results of the study were also recorded.

For the second study, the same interview schedule was administered to a new set of respondents and the same steps were followed to put the respondents at ease and then stimulating the complete response, followed by its recording, objectively.

Sampling Plan

In the first study the sample size of 272 professional was selected by conveniently, choosing 50 professional from each of the five professionals viz. (i) Medicine, (ii) Engineering, (iii) Teaching, (iv) Nursing and (v) Social Work. But because of non-availability of required number of female lawyers only 22 professional could be interviewed, from this category

For the second study also the respondents were selected conveniently choosing 20 professionals from each of the six professions. It was observed that during the collection of data of the law professionals, there were not less than 150-200 lady lawyers practicing in the High Court and Civil Court of Lucknow Bench, thereby reflecting a change in attitude of women towards the profession.

During the first study along with the degree holder engineers most of the engineers had a diploma, whereas, during the 2002 study degree holders were found more in number and in government offices like State Electricity Board and Central Power and Works Department, which was not the case in 1990 study.

In 1990 most of the professionals from the field of engineering were working with UPTRON (public sector unit), which has been closed now and HAL (another PSU) which is not accessible to outsiders now, because of security reasons.

Data Collection

Data was collected for the first study between July 1990 to April 1991 while data collection for the second study was done during the months of November and December 2002.

The researcher went in person to the different institutions and places of work , of all the categories of respondents viz.

- Educational institutions both school and college
- Factories and offices
- Hospitals and clinics
- Courts and tribunals
- Correctional institutions, psychiatric wards and organizations working in the area of social welfare and development

Reliance on Data

For the purpose of the present research, both field and documentary data have been relied upon. Several reference books, field researches and journals have been consulted.

But the findings are heavily based upon the data collected from the field by of the researcher herself.

The collected data have been emphasized upon for of the following reasons:

1. No published research study could be traced out by the researcher, which deals with role conflict among women, especially among those who are professionally qualified. Hence inferences from studies, which are related to the topic, would have resulted in biased conclusions.
2. In research study of this nature, culture of the place where the study is being carried out plays a significant role, prevailing traditions, customs, effects of industrialization and urbanization,

consciousness about economic status etc. are factors of immense important in shaping the personality of an individual.

These factors affect the role-playing demands and expectations from a person in a family and society as a whole. That is to say the same research study may have yielded different result at different types of places like a metropolitan city or a small town.

3. Lastly, observation of face to face reactions and documenting of spontaneous reflexes and information can not be over looked in the context of the present study.

Limitations of the study

1. To streamline the research, respondents from only six professions were chosen. To encounter varied situations, professions like teaching and medicine, where female professionals are found in abundance were chosen. Nursing has been traditionally women oriented profession, social work by trained professionals being a relatively new profession, engineering and law are male dominated and challenging professions for women in India.

To get a uniform and manageable data the number of respondents from each profession was also restricted to 50 professions from each of the six professions for the first study. But unfortunately 50 female professionals from the field of law could not be traced in Lucknow city at the time of data collection for the first study in 1990, so the researcher had to be contented with only 22 lady lawyers.

2. Again, because 50 degree holding female engineers were not available in Lucknow for the first study, the researcher had to consider diploma holders as well, for the study. In the same way non-availability of 50 professionally qualified and trained social workers led to inclusion of females employed in institutions related to the field of social work, but had underdone some specialized training for the job.

3. To have a comparative study, data has to be collected from the same place from where the earlier data was collected. In the second study, the sample size was reduced to 120, so that the study could be completed within the available time, during the second phase of data collection(2002).

   The work was completed in a short span of time but care was taken that it should not affect the quality of data collection. The only difference was that, not much in depth interaction could take place with the respondents which happened during the earlier phase.

4. In some of the options, the frequency was less than 5 in number which makes the relevance of applying Chi. Square test less significant.

5. Because of the time constraint, many professionals available from one organisation were interviewed. The divergence in work environment could not be obtained.

6. The second study being a time-bound study had to be finished within the specific period. The sample size had to be restricted to lower limits(20 each), so as to keep it manageable.

7. In social research percentage of human error in understanding and recording the responses and in tabulation of the data can not be ruled out.

Thus every research study has its own limitations due to its scope, methodology adopted, responses elicited etc. A research study of this nature can present a partial look at certain parts of the picture, which when viewed from a different angle may reveal something different.

References

1. Backwell Dictionary of Sociology (2nd edition) 2000, p. 309.
2. Ibid p. 263.
3. Elliot Merill : Social Disorganisation, Harper and Brother, New York ,1976 , p 09.

4. Lexicon Universal Encyclopaedia, New York, Lexicon publication, vol. 16, p. 271

5. Penguin Dictionary of Psychology, 1986, p. 650.

6. The Dictionary of Family Psychology and Family Therapy 1993, p. 343.

7. Ibid p. 340.

8. Penguin Dictionary of Sociology, 1986, p. 182.

9. Blackwell Dictionary of Sociology, 2000, p. 264.

10. Penguin Dictionary of Psychology, 1986, p. 651.

11. Krech David, Crutchfield RS, and Ballachey : Individual in Society, McGraw Hill Books Co., New York 1962.

12. Nadel S F: The Theory of Social Culture, Routledge and Kegan Paul, London. Ltd., 1969, p. 65.

13. Ralph R : Roles and Relationships, Routledge and Kegan Paul, London. 1976, p. 10.

14. Sutherland and Robert : Introductory Sociology, Oxford and IBH Publication Co. Calcutta 1966, p.77.

15. Neera Desai: Women in Modern India, Vela and C.O. Bombay 1957.

16. Wadely Jacobson: Women in India, Manohar Book Society, 1977, p. 91.

17. Chakraborty Krishna : Conflicting World of Working Mother : A Sociological Enquiry, 1978, p.16.

18. Reddy C R: Changing Status of Educated Working Women, B.R. Publishing Corporation, Delhi, 1986, p.101.

19. Jha and Pujari (Ed.) : Indian Women Today Volume 3, Kanishka Publishers, New Delhi, 1996, p.149.

CHAPTER 3

PROFILE OF WORKING PROFESSIONALS

In the past, role of the women was confined to the four-walls of the house as housewives. They were totally dependent on their husbands or other male members of the family. Males were assigned roles of providing food and economic security to them. According to Reddy C.R. (1986 : 23) : *She was thus not only a dependent but also a helper, an automatic subordinate.*[1]

The profound social changes that India has witnessed in the past 50 years or so have affected its entire population. Yet, in some section of its society their impact has been much more marked than in others. Among the middle class urban educated population, these changes have affected women much more than men. *The place of women in the economic life of a country is undergoing far reaching changes everywhere. These changes in terms of diversity appear to be more marked in developing economies which generally happen to be tradition bound.* Ranade and Ram Chandra[2] (1970 : 1).

The changed socio-economic conditions, particularly after independence, have widened opportunities for women's education and employment and have provided them with new avenues to express and assert their equality. As Kapoor (1974 : 10) puts it : *The urban educated middle and upper class working women comprise comparatively of a recent emerging social group which is drawing the attention of laymen as well as of scholars. Its emergence, in itself, is an indication of significant socio-economic and politico-legal changes taking place in our country*[3].

In recent years in international gatherings also women have come into prominence as a result of the changes which have taken place in the scope and character of the economic life of the society. It is generally difficult to give an all correct profile of women in service and other practising professionals; never-the-less, a review of the available data indicates a change in the occupational pattern. Two trends are thus clearly discernible; i.e. concentration of women in teaching and medicine, and recognition of certain low prestige jobs in clerical services, as particularly suited to women.

Type of education	***Percentage of girls***
General	*26 %*
Professional Education	*10 %*
Engineering	*10 %*
Medicine	*21 %*
Teaching	*38 %*

Ref : Ray (Ed.)[4] *(1970 : 50)*

Devi K Uma (2000) has found that in US women constitute 42.5% of the labour force. Soviet Union (Russia) has accomplished its goal of drawing women into work force – 51.00% and in Federal Republic of Germany 50.2% woman are employed where as 38.0 % of the labour force of U.K. is constituted by women. In these nations also the women are generally employed in lower status, clerical grade and service sector.

Singh and Srivastava (2001) quotes the statisties of 1981 census, where 53.19% of the work force were males and 20.84% were females. National Perspective Plan for woman (1988-2000) show 20.21% women representation in total labour force.

Each and every characteristic of working women is of great academic importance. Their every characteristic influence, their role behaviour, age, marital status, type of family, religion, caste, their income, number and age group of children, number of economically dependent members, period of service, motivating persons, decision makers in the family, helpful persons and time period which they are devoting for pursuing their profession, etc. influence their attitudes and working capacity. The detailed study of all such related factors has been presented in this chapter.

Profession

Income and social status of an individual determine his /her opinions and attitudes toward a particular aspect in life. The different professionals related to the study differ from each other in every aspect of their life viz. economic, social and educational status. These variations in turn affect their attitude, social behaviour and opinions towards life patterns.

Respondents have been selected from six professions viz. teaching engineering, law, medicine, nursing and social work. Teaching and social work require a person to have knowledge and skills in establishing good inter-personal relationship with his on her clients. An engineer needs to be physically strong to handle machines and a lady lawyer needs guts to face the challenges of a male dominated profession.

*In 1993-94 women contributed 52.00% of students who were enrolled in faculties of education i.e. teacher's training departments. This is the only discipline where their proportion is higher than that of men students. Even in 1950-51, their proportion was 32.4%, the highest in any discipline in higher education.

Medicine is yet another discipline where they emerge in good per cent i.e. 34.6%.

But now the shift in discipline choices in professional education is seen e.g. law 11.3%, engineering and agriculture (7.8% each) and commerce (23.1). These are disciplines where more women are entering during the past few decades.

Discussions with experts suggest that by now enrollment of women in engineering technology courses has gone up to 16.00% in the polytechnics. The data from the 1950s onwards reflect two trends - -girls are opting for courses in general education, the other shift is one towards engineering/technology courses. *(Source UGC annual reports)*

Table : 3.3

Number of Respondents:	Medicine	Law	Engineering	Teaching	Nursing	Social Work	Total
1990 **2002**	18.38 **16.16**	8.09 **16.66**	18.38 **16.66**	18.38 **16.66**	18.38 **16.66**	13.38 **16.66**	100.00 **100.00**
Age:							
21 – 30 yrs	26.00 **30.00**	27.27 **40.00**	66.00 **15.00**	42.0 **60.00**	22.00 **70.00**	36.00 **40.00**	37.50 **42.50**
31 – 40 yrs	50.00 **20.20**	63.64 **45.00**	32.00 **52.00**	36.00 **10.00**	34.00 -	24.00 **20.00**	37.87 **24.16**
41 – 50 yrs	14.00 **20.00**	9.09 **15.00**	2.00 **35.00**	10.00 **10.00**	30.00 **20.00**	30.00 **20.00**	16.54 **20.00**
51 yrs and above	10.00 **30.00**	- -	- -	10.00 **20.00**	14.00 **10.00**	10.00 **20.00**	8.21 **13.33**
Average (Yrs)	36.00 **47.12**	33.18 **32.5**	28.60 **37.00**	33.80 **34.00**	38.60 **33.00**	36.40 **41.00**	34.59 **37.43**
X^2 $\mathbf{X^2}$	(Cal) = 57.15; (Tab) = 18.31; P < 0.05, df = 10 **39.749 df = 15 p < 0.05**						
Marital Status:							
Married	84.00 **70.00**	59.09 **50.00**	68.00 **90.00**	56.00 **40.00**	66.00 **20.00**	54.00 **60.00**	65.44 **55.00**
Unmarried	12.00 **20.00**	31.82 **30.00**	28.00 -	36.00 **50.00**	10.00 **80.00**	28.00 **30.00**	25.37 **35.00**
Separated	- -	- -	2.00 -	2.00 -	2.00 -	- -	1.10 -
Divorced	2.00 -	- **5.00**	2.00 -	2.00 -	4.00 -	2.00 -	2.21 **0.83**
Widowed	2.00 **10.00**	9.09 **15.00**	- **10.00**	4.00 **10.00**	8.00 -	6.00 **16.0-0**	5.88 **9.16**
X^2 $\mathbf{X^2}$	(Cal) = 14.48) Tab 18.31 p > 0.05; df = 10 **39.792, df=15 p<0.05**						
Religion:							
Hindu	44.00 **95.00**	90.91 **95.00**	90.00 **85.00**	73.00 **56.00**	40.00 **60.00**	43.00 **80.00**	75.37 **80.83**
Muslim	4.00 -	- **5.00**	4.00 -	6.00 **40.00**	12.00 -	6.00 -	5.88 **7.5**
Christian	2.00 -	- -	- -	20.00 -	46.00 **30.00**	-	12.87 **5.00**
Sikh	2 000 -	- -	6.00 -	1.00 **4.00**	2.00 **10.00**	4.00 **20.00**	3.31 **3.33**
Jain	8.00 **5.00**	9.09 -	- **15.00**	- -	- -	2.00 -	2.57 **3.33**
X^2 $\mathbf{X^2}$	Cal = 48.68; (Tab) = 11.07; p<.05; df = 5 **86.725, df=20, p<0.05**						
Type of Family:							
Joint	36.00 **30.00**	40.90 **55.00**	54.00 **50.00**	60.00 **90.00**	38.00 **10.00**	54.00 **40.00**	47.79 **45.83**
Nuclear	64.00 **70.00**	59.10 **45.00**	46.00 **50.00**	40.00 **10.00**	62.00 **90.00**	46.00 **60.00**	52.21 **54.16**
X^2 $\mathbf{X^2}$	Cal = 9.19; (Tab) 11.07; p > 0.05, df = 7 **29.17, df = 5, p < 0.05**						

Distribution of Castes among Hindu Respondents:

	Brahmin	Vaishya	Rajput	Khatri	Kayastha	SC/ OBC	Total
1990	26.83	15.12	12.19	12.19	28.78	4.16	100.00
2002	**29.89**	**17.52**	**5.15**	**8.24**	**26.80**	**12.37**	**100.00**

Number of Children:

None	11.36 **31.25**	28.57 **15.38**	36.11 **-**	18.75 **12.5**	12.50 **-**	16.22 **25.00**	19.21 **15.06**
One Child	18.18 **31.25**	14.29 **23.07**	30.56 **20.00**	28.13 **25.00**	22.50 **50.00**	18.92 **25.00**	22.66 **26.02**
2-3 Children	65.91 **37.5**	42.85 **61.53**	33.33 **80.00**	43.75 **50.00**	52.50 **50.00**	40.54 **50.00**	47.78 **57.53**
More than 3 Children	4.55 **-**	14.29 **-**	- **-**	9.37 **12.5**	12.50 **-**	24.32 **-**	10.35 **1.36**
Average	2.01 **1.00**	1.79 **1.20**	1.14 **1.40**	1.75 **1.50**	2.04 **1.25**	2.18 **1.00**	1.83 **1.20**
X^2 (Cal) = 9.19 ; (Tab)= (11.09) ; $p > 0.05$; df =5 **X^2 41.3 df = 15 $P < 0.05$**							

Age group of the children of the respondents:

	Up to 2 yrs	3-6 yrs	7-14 yrs	above 14 yrs	Total
1990 **2002**	8.56 **8.06**	29.28 **16.12**	33.33 **40.38**	28.83 **35.44**	100.00 **100.00**

Period of Service:

	Medicine	Law	Engineering	Teaching	Nursing	Social Work	Total
Just Joined	- **-**	9.09 **5.00**	6.00 **-**	8.00 **-**	- **5.00**	2.00 **-**	3.68 **1.66**
Less than a year	10.00 **-**	- **-**	2.00 **-**	14.00 **20.00**	- **-**	- **20.00**	4.78 **6.66**
1 - 3 years	8.00 **40.00**	9.09 **30.00**	8.00 **-**	14.00 **30.00**	4.00 **50.00**	20.00 **10.00**	10.66 **26.66**
3 - 5 years	8.00 **-**	- **20.00**	26.00 **-**	8.00 **10.00**	2.00 **10.00**	6.00 **10.00**	9.19 **8.33**
above 5 years	74.00 **60.00**	81.82 **45.00**	58.00 **100.00**	56.00 **40.00**	94.00 **35.00**	72.00 **60.00**	71.69 **56.66**
Average	11.1 **9.9**	12.27 **5.2**	8.7 **10.0**	8.4 **4.6**	14.1 **4.9**	11.44 **6.7**	11.36 **6.9**
X^2 X^2	Cal =23.46; Tab = 11.07, $p < 0.05$; df = 5 **49.62 df = 20 $p < 0.05$**						

Monthly income

Below 2000	30.00 **-**	59.10 **30.00**	72.00 **-**	62.00 **20.00**	94.00 **-**	76.00 **-**	67.27 **8.33**
2001-5000	52.00 **-**	31.80 **45.00**	28.00 **-**	26.00 **30.00**	6.00 **70.00**	22.00 **10.00**	27.21 **25.83**
5001-10,000	18.00 **20.00**	9.09 **15.00**	- **45.00**	6.00 **40.00**	- **-**	2.00 **60.00**	5.52 **28.33**
10,000 & above	- **90.00**	- **10.00**	- **55.00**	- **10.00**	- **30.00**	- **30.00**	- **37.50**
Average Rs.	3585 **21,750**	2556.8 **10,875**	2220 **11,625**	1980 **5,850**	1515 **8,050**	2020 **9,350**	2287.68 **11,2500**
X^2 X^2	(Cal) =107.48; (Tab) = 18.31 $p < 0.05$ df 10 **95.849 df= 15 $p < 0.05$**						

Note : All figures show percentage. Percentage as the top refers to 1990 study and the second figure in bold is that of 2002.

The first study was undertaken for the purpose of pursuing Ph.D. The aim was to study the role conflict among working women professionals. To keep the size of the sample manageable, and also keeping in view the accuracy of the results, it was decided to select fifty professionals from each of the six professions of medicine, law, engineering, teaching, nursing and social work. The number of practising lady lawyers within the corporation limits of Lucknow city was not even fifty, and thus only twenty two respondents could be contacted.

The second study was undertaken with the purpose of assessing the change brought about by the rapid pace of urbanisation, industrialisation and globalization with respect to conflicts faced by the working professionals, in the past decade since 1990. Thus, it was thought that a sample size of 120 respondents should be able to get the desired effect, for the study. Twenty respondents from each of the six professions were interviewed, making the total sample size 120.

Unlike during the earlier study, the number of practising lady lawyers has grown phenomenally and there were no less than 150-200 lady lawyers alone in the High Court, and lower courts, leave alone their tribunals, from where the data was primarily collected.

According to YWCA survey of 1993, in 1990 only 17.00% of the professional, technical and related workers were women, of whom 3/4th were teachers. The percent of women to men in selected professionals are, physicians and surgeons 7.1%, lawyers 2.1%, teachers 30.3%, nursing and other health technicians 72.2%, and scientists 10.9%. In 1971, out of 6,000 trained social workers, 30.00% were found to be women.

Age Composition

Age as a variable, is important in any study of the present nature, because a person acquires experience with advancement in age, learns new things, modifies old values, and defies certain generalization regarding external relatives. Various types of responsibilities which a person is supposed to discharge also depend upon the age of a person. Here, we may refer to Talwar (1984:14). *Age influence the capacity to work*[1].

The table reveals that over a period of time professionals getting into the practice have become younger in age (maximum percentage in the age group of 21-30 yrs), whereas in the first study, maximum percentage was from 31-40 years age group. On an average, engineers

(28.60 yrs) were the youngest of the lot, while in the second study, lawyers are the youngest respondents (32.5yrs.). But, the average age of the respondents, from all the six professions, have gone up from 34.59 years to 37.50 years.

Thus an average female professional is still a middle aged woman, advanced in age by a few years over the last study done. On applying X^2 test on the data, the studies show that the two variables of age and profession bear a significant relationship. Infact it is found to be highly related in 2002 study ($p = 0.000494$)

Marital status

Marital status has a very significant role to play in the life of an individual and more so in case of a woman. Ours is a patriarchial society where the woman is expected to adjust to the new environment of her husband's family that i with her in-laws.

Different marital status entails different set of roles, to a woman. Marriage multiplies the roles a woman has to play. This multiplicity of roles leads to a variety of obligations and duties, which she has to fulfil during her life time For a professional, woman by simple mathematics, one can say, that diversified roles encompassing multiple duties and responsibilities lead to different kinds of conflicts. Diagrammatically it can be shown as in **Fig. 3.2.**

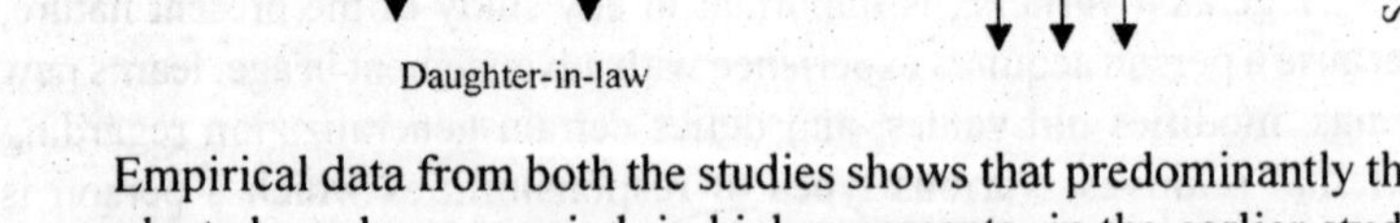

Empirical data from both the studies shows that predominantly the respondents have been married, in higher percents in the earlier study (65.44), than in the later study (55.00). The percent of unmarried professionals pluging into the professional pursuit has shown an increase of 10.00%, reflecting that more women want to take up work before getting married. Divorced professionals are seen to be more evenly distributed among various professions in the first study (the only profession having divorced respondents, is law in the later study).

Widows are seen to be surfacing in even distribution in both the studies. It is generally seen that divorced or widowed women take up jobs due to economic necessity, so as to remain financially independent. During the second study, it was observed that a few of the respondents were married for the second time, reflecting acceptability of divorced professionals for remarriage.

The result of chi square test show that in case of 1990 data, the two attributes of marital status and profession of the respondent bear no association, whereas in 2002, the two attributes show a highly significant relationship.

Religion

Although India is a secular country, but all the same, religion has been a predominant force for different activities and behaviour in our society. Once upon a time, there were some professions which were looked down by the people, following a particular religion, but the people from other religions gave a dignified sanction for pursuing the same, a notebale example being that of the nursing profession. But, the collected data shows that such notions governed by religion, have become mellowed in the society. This is mainly for the want of increase in the family income, and salaried women's assertion to become financially independent. *Johanson (1979) avers that the members of professional groups are drawn mostly from upper class and dominant ethenic group. (Kalbagh 1992 : 150)*[5]. In the present studies also Hindu respondent are in great majority.

Religion, as history shows, is labelled as a weakening force for social development and progress. But in the present studies religion surfaces as a weak force in equality for the choice of the profession. *But* Kumar Hazira (2000 : 19) quotes National commission for Women Report 2000 that *only 16.00 % of Muslim Women are employed as compared to 31.00% hindu and 37.0% Christian women*[6]. The percentage of Muslim respondents is low in the present studies also.

Respondents in both the studies have been Hindus, in overwhelming majority (75.37 and 80.83%). Muslim professionals in highest percent, were in the teaching profession, in 2002 (40.00); in the earlier study of 1990, maximum number of Muslim professionals were in the field of nursing (12.00). The percentage of the Muslim professionals has increased from 5.88% to 7.5%, while Christian professionals are predominantly practicing nursing, and their representation in the sample also reduced from 12.87% to 5.00%.

X^2 calculations in both the studies show association between the two variables of religion followed by the respondent and the profession she is pursuing.

Caste distribution

In ancient Indian society caste of an individual played a significant role in carrying out any profession. Aryans followed 'Varna' system according to different castes in society and associated these various castes with different professions. Thus, profession was assigned according to the birth/*varna* of an individual.

But, over a period of time, with the advent of education society has broadened its outlook. People choose their profession because of their interest or circumstances. In olden times, women of only lower castes used to work outside the premises of their houses, carrying the traditional work of their women - ancestors. These were low paid jobs, almost on the items of transaction in kind. Such work didn't require any education or formal training, and their skill sets, such as they were, passed from one generation to another.

When the country became independent Contitution of India provided provision for the upliftment of the backward classes, that is, reservation in jobs and reservations in educational institutions etc. Other constitutional rights and safeguards were forther granted to bring this section of the society at par with the upper classes.

During the course of conducting of both the studies, the respondents were found to be belonging to the castes commonly seen in the city of Lucknow. Earlier, the Kayastha were more in percentage, but in the latter study, the Brahmin respondents were found in maximum numbers. There is a substantial increase in the representation of respondents from the scheduled castes, and other backward classes, which is quite a laudable achievement. The caste distribution of the respondents in the two studies is shown in the Table 3.1 page 33. The empirical derivation is different from documented derivations.

The survey on higher education undertaken by the National Commission on Teachers, compares the enrollment of the schedule caste students in general courses, and in professional courses. It notes that between 1964-65 to 1977-78, there was an increase in the enrollment in general courses, whereas it declined in the professional courses. By 1996-97, only 2.4% enrollment of SC women took place in comparison to the total enrollment for the year.

Another fact noted while collecting the data was that all the Muslim respondents belong to sunni sect of Islam and all the Christian respondents were Protestants.

Mukherjee (R.K. 1961: 57) opines that *caste has become so significant in Indian social structure that a meaningful study is not possible without it being taken into account*[7]. On the contrary, the collected data reveals that the major castes are so evenly distributed and represented in all the six profession, that the impact of caste on the profession seems to be in cognizable.

Type of Family

Traditionally, the Indian society has largely consisted up of joint families. But, because of the impact of urbanization and industrialization, nuclear families came into existence. Later, westernization also played a role in the emergence of nuclear families in the cities of the country.

Now-a-days, because of independent thoughts and values of the younger generation, we find more incidences of nuclear families in big cities. Housing in flats have also contributed to the emergence of nuclear families, with parents living in the same city.

Respondents, in both the studies, have been from nuclear families in greater numbers. Widening marginally, showing a trend of increasing inclinations towards nuclear family system.

In 2002, only in the teaching community, an overwhelming majority of respondents came from the joint family (90.00), making it the most convenient profession for women even in a joint family system. Nursing professionals were found to be living in nuclear family, in maximum percentage (90.00), Most of the nurses were found to be unmarried, living in a rented accodomation or a hostel provided by the employing institutions.

Application of X^2 test upon 1990 data shows a non-significant relationship, while in 2002, it bears a significant relationship.

Number of Children

With the coming of children in the family the responsibility of the family members multiply. The role of the mother becomes much more important because children look for mental, emotional and psychological support in the mother first and when not properly taken care of by her, go to other family members. Lack of such support leads to behavioural problems, and in recent years, this has even led to perverted behaviour eg., addiction to drugs, pornography, etc.

For a working woman, who has to devote a good number of hours to her profession, the role of a mother becomes all the more challenging and needs proper tunning both inside and outside. With the cooperation of other family members and her insight of human psychology, she may be able to perform her job perfectly to the satisfaction of her family members, as well as to her own self.

Geeta Mukerjee (1978: 104) writes, *Education of woman may not influence fertility directly. But in combination with other factors viz. occupation, income, social position etc., it acts as a most favourable and satisfactory inhibitor in bringing down fertility*[8]. The result of the two studies shows concurrence with this observation.

Respondents in maximum numbers, have 2 or 3 children (47.78 and 57.53)*, with the percentage showing a marginal increase only in teaching community who have more than 3 children.

Percentage of respondents with one child has also gone up, pointing towards the trend of having less number of children, ending responsibilities upon the professional related to child rearing. Thus reflecting that with the professional pursuit, the size of the family has to be small.

The average number of children in both the studies is less than 2 (earlier 1.83, later 1.2) Thus, Geeta Mukerjee's observation holds true even in contemporary times.

Results of chi square test on 1990 data show that the two variables– number of children, and the profession of the respondent, bear no

* Figures in parenthesis shows comparision of two studies.

significant relationship, while on 2002 data, the test shows association between the two variables.

Period of Service

Practical experience tells us that with time, everything gets adjusted. Going out of the house for a good number of hours in a day disturbs the routine of the whole family. But, with the passage of time, the family members get attuned to the new routine and the woman also makes the necessary adjustments in her work schedule at home. Thus, the number of years devoted to the profession, becomes important in the study of role conflict.

In both the studies, although respondents in maximum percents have been working for more than 5 years, in the second study this percentage has come down considerably (from 71.69 to 56.66). A good number of respondents in the later study (26.66), have been in the profession for 1 - 3 years which is quite a high percentage from the earlier study (10.66). The average period of service, in most of the professions have also come down the only exception being that of engineering, where the average period of service of engineering professionals has increased from 8.7 years to 10.0 years.

The overall average of period of service also came down from 11.36 years to 6.9 years, in the later study. Results of Chi Square Test, when applied on the two sets of data, show an association between the period of service and the profession of the respondent.

Monthly Income

After the satisfaction of the professional herself, next comes the finances generated in the job, which attracts an individual to a particular profession. In the present times, it has in fact become the foremost consideration when it comes to choosing a profession. This fact was reflected by some of the respondents, during informal talks, and has been clearly stated by others, in the study itself.

Ever growing number of educated Indian women are entering the field of employment and under the pressure of a growing economic crisis many families expect of their women that they contribute to the maintenance of the family.

Now-a-days, it is seen, that ever if there are a little inconvienences, because of the job of a woman member in the family she gets mutualy adjusted as she brings in a fat salary, which ultimately suppliment the gross income of the house. Many a times, cases have come to the notice that girl's employment becomes an added consideration for her marriage so as to maintain a good standard of living beside elevating the family's social and economic status.

For the purpose of the present study, the respondent is not considered as the bread-earner of the family, but in light of the above mentioned facts, income of the respondent becomes one of the major considerations for the practice of the profession. Interpretation of the gathered data show the following results.

There is a stark difference in the monthly income of the respondents. In 1990, maximum percent of respondents were earning less than Rs. 2000 (67.27), whereas the maximum percent (37.50) of the respondents are reported to be earning more than Rs. 10,000/- in the later study. Only law and teaching professionals were found to be earning less than Rs.2000/- per month.

The average income of the total respondents of the later study (11,250) is almost 5 times that of earlier study (Rs. 2,287.68). Thus, the earning capacity of a professionally qualified woman has shown a significant increase over a period of ten years.

Considerations for undergoing the professional training

It is a difficult choice to make for a person as to what career he/she would take up in the course of life. But after concentrating on the aims of life, and other alied circumstances, one can come to a conclusion regarding the choice of a career or profession.

Gertude William, (1945: 62) way back remarked; *The stay at home girls is fast becoming an anachorsim and will soon be as extinct-as the dodo. Parents cannot afford to keep their daughters idle. Many parents now recognize that a professional qualification is a form of insurance against future economic mishap even if their daughters do marry*[9].

Throwing light on the factors which persuade a woman to choose a particular profession, it will be a help in ascertaining as to what may be the guiding factors for the choice of her profession. Is it the personal interest, or simply the tradition in the family, or whether the choice is guided by its earnings etc.

Table : 3.3 : Considerations for undergoing the professional training

Considerations	1990	2002	Personal interest in the profession					
Personal interest in the profession	54.78	**57.66**	Med	Law	Eng.	Tea.	Nur	S.W.
			88.00	27.27	54.00	44.00	68.0	32.00
			45.00	**40.00**	**55.00**	**58.00**	**55.0**	**65.00**
Easy availability of admission	14.70	**17.50**						
Good prospects of earning money	18.01	**1.66**						
Family tradition	11.40	**6.66**						
Any other	27.21	**25.83**						
Base	100.00	**100.00**						

Other considerations are:

Medicine

- Husband studying medicine at the time of marriage and she followed suit.
- Parents wanted for name and fame
- Parents' ambition
- Has a good career

Law

- From competition point of view
- Suited astrologically
- Friends joined it
- Took it as a challenge to get justice to others
- Took it as a challenge - for legal literacy
- To get the hostel accommodation

Teaching

- To get out of home
- Forced by school authorities

Nursing

- Uniform attracted (20 respondents in 1990)
- Wanted any professional qualification
- When child fell sick and faced problems at the hospital
- To take care of the sick mother
- For economic independence after parent's death. (Stipend was paid during nursing training way back in 60.'s)
- For financial independence after divorce
- Serve others
- Motivated by a film

Engineering

- For technical training
- To accept a challenging profession

Social Work

- Forced by family circumstances to take up work
- To remain independent

Both the studies show that personal interest in the profession was the main consideration in choosing the profession (54.78 and 57.66), followed by the category of individual considerations, of the respondents (27.21 and 25.83).

These individual reasons provide a good insight into the matter as to what may trigger an individual to shape the course of her life. However, it also strengthen the notion that at times some incidents leave such an impression on people that it has lasting impact on their life. Some choose their profession on such flimsy pretexts like getting a hostel, or to get the company of friends !

The study further reveals that the choice of profession in not guided by the religion followed by any person. An overwhelming majority of respondents among Hindu (53.66 and 53.00), Muslim (62.50 and 66.6), Christian (68.57 and 66.66), and Jain (71.43 and 100), community, cited their personal interest (55.88 and 54.99) as the motivational force for going for the professional training. For sikhs respondents even after more than a decade, reasons for choosing the profession remain largely same - easy availability of admission (33.33 and 50.00), and other personal reasons (33.33 and 50.00). For respondents of other communities also easy availability of the admission was also a reason given by a considerable number (14.34 and 17.50), showing an increase in percentage. While earning prospects as a choice to go for any profession (17.64 and 5.00) has lost its weight over a period of time.

A great number of respondents stated that they were self motivated to choose the profession of their choice (50.73 and 52.50), whereas the father stands out as the second potent, motivating person (30.15 and 25.00), followed by the mother (19.85 and 9.06), but the percentages of respondents waned over a period of time.

Thus, it can be concluded that most of the professionals joined the profession, out of their own interest; were self motivating, and were not guided by the religion in adoption of their profession.

Stage of adoption of professional practice

It becomes an important factor, in the light of the fact as to what made the woman follow the profession, for which she is qualified - is it to make use of her qualifications or because of economic compulsions, or to utilise her leisure time?

In good majority of cases (63.97 and 83.33), the respondents took up professional practice before they got married, and have been in their professional pursuit, even after they got married. Infact, in almost all cases, the respondents took up the practice of the profession immediately after the completion of their course of study.

When respondents started their professional practice after marriage (26.47 and 15.00), most of them were studying at the time of marriage, and consequently, their practice commenced after marriage. In a small percent only, respondents took up the practice of the profession, after their children started going to the school (8.07 and 1.66). In the earlier study, this category got represented by respondents from medicine (12.00), law (27.27), teaching (10.00), and social work (10.09); where as, in the latter one, only law professionals (10.0) represented this category. In the earlier study, a few more circumstances were stated for taking up their professional pursuit, after a long gap. These were, after retirement of the husband (2.00 from teaching), after the children were married off (2.00 teaching), after the death of the husband (2.00 from nursing) or after their divorce (2.00 from nursing).

On application of X^2 test, it was found that on 1990 data, X^2 cal = 28.15, tab = 11.07 $P < 0.05$ df = 15 which shows significance between the two variables. On the 2002 data, X^2 is equal to 22.75, df = 10 and $P < 0.05$ which again shows a significant relationship between stage of adoption of professional practice and the profession of the respondent which is not supported by the field data.

Causes for taking up the professional practice

This was to study the reasons which led to the use of their educational attainment. This question becomes all the more relevant to the study, as it has already been stated and analysed that respondents had an underlying idea or aim which propelled them into the study of the professional course. So, at the time of practice, are they fulfilling those aims and objectives, or because of change in values with time and experiences in life, have they different reasons for taking up the professional practice ?

Promilla Kapoor (1974 : 56) writes that *the studies have pointed out that it is not only those who are extremely hard pressed, by dire economic necessity, who get out of their homes to take up gainful employment, and that, the scene has changed considerably over time*[10]

In Verma's study (1964), 42.5 % of women were found to be working, owing to various other reasons than economic necessity, whereas, 57.5% took up employment only due to economic necessity. Srivastava (1986), in her research, found as many as 40% of her sample of urban educated women reporting that they worked for non-economic advantages.

Kapur (1970) found that 18.00 % of the married women were working mainly because of their interest in their profession or jobs, and 9.00 % were in employment because of their ambition for a career, or to achieve a position or status of their own.

Data collected from both the studies have been tabulized as under :

Table : 3.4 : Causes for taking up the professional practice by their profession

Cause	Medicine	Law	Engineering	Teaching	Nursing	Social work
Need for adding to the family income	26.00 -	45.45 **34.00**	42.00 -	24.00 **40.00**	48.00 **30.00**	40.00 **30.00**
Availability of free time	14.00 -	27.27 **35.00**	14.00 -	38.00 **40.00**	15.00 **10.00**	34.00 **10.00**
To avoid confrontation at home	2.00 -	9.09 -	6.00 -	6.00 -	16.00 -	10.00 -
Desire to be free from dependence	30.00 **40.00**	36.36 **35.00**	28.00 **60.00**	46.00 **40.00**	80.00 **70.00**	42.00 **40.00**
To avoid wastage of professional talent	92.00 **60.00**	81.82 **4.00**	61.00 **40.00**	50.00 -	82.00 **16.00**	30.00 **20.00**
To get rid of the overburden of household chores	2.00 -	- -	6.00 -	- -	16.00 -	4.00 -
Husband forced her	- -	4.54 -	2.00 -	- -	- -	- -
Base	100.00 **100.00**	100.00 **100.00**	100.00 **100.00**	100.00 **100.00**	100.00 **100.00**	100.00 **100.00**

The economic factor remains the main consideration for women being in employment. In a London School of Economics' (LSE) Social Sciences Department Report, (Women Wife and Worker), says – *Respondents' main reasons for taking up employment was financial reason – to add to their family economy – higher standard of living for their families, more varied diet, durable consumer goods, pocket – money and toys to the children.*

Companionship to be found in the factory which contrasted favourably with the isolation of life at home, was not cited as the main consideration; work not a escape from family but a means of assisting it'' (L.S.E. Report 1960 : 6).

The result of the collected data concurs with the findings of Kapoor that it is not the economic compulsions which drives these women to work. It however is in contradiction with Ranade & Ram Chandran's study (1970 : 3), which says that *women from lower income group take up jobs mainly with the view to support or supplement family income.* The same study says, (p. 5) *that women coming from higher income group families are motivated to take up jobs for utilization of leisure, use of vocational training and desire to have their own money.*[12]

It was to avoid wastage of professional talent (69.85) in the earlier study, which made a large majority of women take up professional practice. But, in the later study, only medical practitioners held it responsible as a driving force in taking up their professional pursuit (60.00 of the medical respondents). The predominant factor, which evolved as a single largest motivating factor for the respondent, in the second study is the desire to remain free from financial dependence (47.50), which was stated by a good percent of respondents in 1990 also (49.63); so, it can be concluded that professional woman of today wants to be financially independent, irrespective of the profession which she is practicing. Respondents in good number, especially in the earlier study, came out for work as an 'escape mechanism' from either work load, or confrontation at home.

Motivators for professional practice

Action or behaviour of an individual depends on the degree of motivation provided to him/her. If the motivating force is strong enough to give impetus to an individual, the person gains moral support too, to pursue the desired work.

There are mainly three types of motivators; self motivators, other motivators and situational motivations. There is yet another type of motivator, viz., the primary motivators. We come across on radio, television, films and even in magazines that today, women in India are openly advocating about women emancipation, and its can only be brought assent by economic independence. Gone are the days when women were puppets in the hands of males in the society. The need to achieve this type of aim, through self-consciousness serve as 'primary motivation'. Such motivating forces singly, and sometimes jointly, inspire an individual to move in the desired fashion and path. A strong force, in the form of any of these motivators, can pull out women from their custom-bound, traditional roles in the society.

We can't over look the role of education, which gives the women of today a confidence to go out and fight for their rights, and cast a niche for themselves. Education also gives them the understanding of equal rights and privileges in the society. It has always been a basic factor in their emancipation.

On compiling the collected data to find out who had been the motivating force behind respondents' taking up their professional practice, the following picture emerges.

In both the studies, the motivating force behind the single largest group of respondents to go for professional practice has been their own self (61.40 and 62.50), which is irrespective of the profession of the respondent - medicine (56.00 and 65.00), law (45.45 and 40.0), engineering (64.00 and 70.00), teaching (58.0 and 50.00), nursing (84.00 and 80.00), and social work (52.00 and 70.00). Percentages of the respondents from each of the six profession show more or less the same trend, in the present study as was in the earlier one, except in case of the profession of social work, where the percent has shown much improvement. Father, (21.32 and 17.50), and mother (16.91 and 13.32), have been the other driving force for adoption of professional practice followed by the husband (4.78) in the earlier study.

Another interesting aspect which has emerged out of the two studies is two fold i.e., when the professional has started her professional practice after marriage, and after the children started going to the school. In both the cases the husband (100.00), has been the motivating force, reflecting the change of mind set of the males in the society. These husbands (read males) want their spouses to be more productive towards their societal responsibilities.

Here, economic pressure of the family, or higher materialistic status, may be the idea behind the scene. In some of the cases, it is also reported that the husband being too much engaged in his work, cannot give enough time to his wife at home. Then, out of need for positive change in environment the husband, knowing his wife's talent and capacity, motivated her to go for professional practice (instances cited by respondents from law and teaching professions).

Decision Maker in the Family

Decision making is a vital activity. The success of an endeavor depends on whether the decision taken was the right one or not. Thus, the decision making becomes an important factor in the smooth running of family affairs. The role of the decision maker becomes all the more significant, as he or she is the pivotal person around whom all the important activities in the family revolve.

Traditionally, the role of the decision maker was played by the eldest male member in the family, and his decisions were taken as the final word, without any questioning. With the forming of nuclear families, the role was passed on to the male bread-earner of the family. As he was the provider of daily necessities to his family, his wishes and decisions couldn't be challenged.

But, with the change in situation, where women are also equally sharing the financial burden of the family, they are also commanding a say in the decision making process in the family. Today, it is generally seen that the person who controls the finances of the family takes the decision for the family. *Studies of Blood and Wolfe (1960) Dupri (1969), Safilios-Rothschild (1970), Bahr (1974), Mc Donald (1980) and Ferber (1982) have found that employed women have more decision making powers*[13] *(Ramu 1989 : 159).* We also see more and more incidences of sharing of decisions making, in the family in this study.

In joint families, in keeping with the traditions, the wishes and decisions of the elder members are not ignored by the young ones. But the wishes of the younger lot are also not overlooked, and taken into consideration by the elder members, thus more or less making joint compromised decisions.

In the nuclear family, the husband and wife jointly take decisions for the family. Where children are grown up, and are involved in any particular situation they are also encouraged to make decisions. This is a healthy trend as decision-making is a vital exercise. But, if children are involved from an early age, they grow up as more confident adults.

Table : 3.5 : Persons taking decision by the profession

Persons taking decision	Medicine	Law	Engineering	Teaching	Nursing	Social work	Total
Self	86.0 **80.00**	90.91 **95.00**	66.00 **100.00**	76.00 **50.00**	76.00 **60.00**	48.00 **60.00**	72.06 **74.16**
Husband	26.00 **60.00**	45.45 **35.00**	46.00 **65.00**	38.00 **40.00**	44.00 **20.00**	40.00 **50.00**	44.12 **45.00**
Mother	- **10.00**	- **20.00**	14.00 -	14.00 **35.00**	- **20.00**	2.00 **20.00**	5.88 **19.16**
Father	4.00 **10.00**	- **20.00**	10.00 -	22.00 **35.00**	2.00 **20.00**	10.00 **20.00**	10.66 **19.16**
Mother-in-law	- **10.00**	- -	12.00 -	- -	6.00 **10.00**	4.00 -	4.04 **3.53**
Father-in-law	2.00 **10.00**	- -	- -	2.00 -	2.00 **10.00**	8.00 -	2.94 **3.33**
Any other person	2.00 **10.00**	- **10.00**	2.00 -	2.00 -	2.00 -	4.00 -	2.20 **3.33**

Both the studies clearly reveal that the woman herself is involved in decision making mechanics, in the family (72.06 and 74.16) and there has been an increase in their percentage. All the engineering respondents (100.00) reported that they are part of the decision making in their family in 2002. The finding here concurs with what Sood (1991 : 91) has to say that, *compared to the past working women have better say in the decision making structures of the family.*[14]

From the economic factor associated with the additional income of the respondents, it is worth recalling, that such professionals are more intelligent than an average person. And also she being the one with better foresight and judgment of situation because of her exposure to a wider forum, she is able to take decisions which are helpful for the family, and thereby becoming an integral part of the decision making authority. This also has a bearing on the fact that the working professional is more assertive with regard to taking decision by the family.

Decision Maker in the Family and Type of Family

This is to study whether there is any set pattern like the traditional one where the eldest in the family takes decision for the family, and for each and every member individually as well, or has our society adopted the modern outlook where decisions are joint, and further modernisation leading to individuals taking decisions for themselves. The collected data are assimilated in the table 3.6.

Table : 3.6 : Decision Maker in the Family by Type of Family

Decision Maker	Joint	Nuclear	Total
Self	32.31	39.44	36.03
	14.54	**50.76**	**34.16**
Husband	11.54	20.42	16.18
	-	**7.64**	**4.16**
Mother	3.58	-	1.84
	12.72	**12.30**	**12.5**
Father	10.77	2.11	6.25
	12.72	**9.23**	**10.83**
in-laws	13.08	-	6.24
	3.63	-	**1.66**
Joint decisions	24.60	38.03	31.62
	61.81	**26.15**	**42.5**

The table shows that irrespective of the type of the family they come from, the respondents have been involved in decision making for the family. In both the studies, representation is more from nuclear family (39.44 and 50.76), and over the period of more than 10 years, the working professionals have become more assertive. If we look from another perspective, this can also be assessed as, the people of the family are more willing to accept what the working professional has to say, leading to an increase in the acceptability of the women professionals in the matter of family decision. In joint families, joint decisions have become more acceptable. Showing, thereby, the breaking up of the patriarchal hierarchy of the joint family, which in earlier times was supposed to be the nucleus for taking decisions for all the family members.

The percentage of joint decision increased almost three times (24.60 to 61.81), in joint family, thereby reflecting a shift in the patriarchal family values of the society.

Joint decisions have become less popular in nuclear family (38.03 and 26.15), and have shown a downward trend. Husband's involvement is also in a small percent only, in the recent study (7.6) which is much lower in percentage than that of the study conducted earlier (20.42).

Here the professional herself emerges as a competant and quite acceptable instrument in the mechanism of decision making, irrespective of the type of family to which she belongs.

Thus we see the change in the attitude of the society, where a qualified woman who is a responsible person at the place of work, takes decisions for herself, and also in the family matters. Joint decisions are also a step forward, where the eldest in the family accepts the decision by consensus.

Persons providing help in household chores

Traditionally, it was the sole duty of the women folk of the house to take care of household duties and responsibilities, whereas the males in the family were expected to do jobs which generally required going out of the premises of the house. It was considered derogatory on the part of either of the two parties, if they were not able to do their part of the work.

With the growing influence of western culture on our society and concept of nuclear family, the distinction of work on traditional lines is becoming narrower and narrower. With the wife also going out for equal hours of a day for work, it became obligatory for the husband to share her domestic responsibilities too. Children are also required to be more independent and helpful, contributing their mite.

In such a situation, it was all the more necessary to include in the purview of this research study, this aspect of additional help to the respondents. The gathered data show that the respondents in large percents get help from their husbands (32.72 and 30.83), followed by their mother (18.38 and 19.16), mother-in-law (16.18) in 1990, and son (13.32) in the 2002.

In the later study more percentage has emerged claiming help from the sons (13.32), than the from daughters (10.83); the earlier study showed the traditional expectation, daughter (16.54), helping in more numbers, than the sons (11.03). Again, this reflects the change of societal attitudes towards the traditional roles played in the family by the sons and the daughters. Other people who have been found to be helpful towards the professionals are father (9.93 and 12.50), sister (5.88 and 3.33), and other persons (13.23 and 9.99). The percent of respondents receiving no help at all has also decreased (from 21.32 to 18.33), showing that the family takes cognizance of the fact that the women is working, and needs a helping hand in taking up her household responsibilities.

Extent of help

Maximum percent of respondents getting much help are those whose husbands provide help (37.58) in the earlier study, and mothers provide much help in the later study (40.38). From earlier to the later study, husband and mother have changed places in providing much help to the working professional. More mother's are providing much help (36.53) in the latter study than in the earlier one (26.75).

Sons are providing much help in less percentage in the present study, than in the earlier on (15.92 and 11.53). Daughters provided much help in greater percentage in 1990 study (20.38), than in the present one (14.6). In 1990 19.85% and in 2002 15.00% of the total respondents did not receive any kind of help in doing house jobs, from their family members.

It can be concluded that the two entities in the family i.e. the husband and the mother remains the two most helpful persons for the professional while children also help the working mother. A good percent of sons and daughters, and also the husband, accept and extend help in whatever way, much or little, to the working professional, thereby making an attempt to lessen the burden upon the shoulder of the working professional.

References

1. Reddy, C.R. : Changing Status of Educated Working Women, B.R. Publishing Corp. Delhi, 1986, p. 23.

2. Ranade and Ram Chandran : Women and Employment TISS study, 1970, p. 1.

3. Kapoor, Promilla : The Changing Status of Working Women in India, Vikas Publishing House, New Delhi, 1974, p. 56.

4. Talwar, Usha : Social Profile of Working Women, Jain Brothers, Jodhpur, 1984, p. 14.

5. Kalbagh, C. (ed) : Woman in Enterprises and profession, Discovery Publishing House, New Delhi, 1992, p. 150.

6. Kumar, Hazira (ed) : Status of Muslim Women in India Aakas Books, New Delhi, 2000, p. 19.

7. Mukherjee, R.K. : The Horizon of Marriage, Asia Publishing House, Delhi, 1961, p. 57.

8. Mukherjee, Geeta : Indian Working Class, Asia Publishing House, Delhi, 1978, p. 104.

9. William, Gertude : Woman at Work, Nicholson and Watson, London, 1945, p. 62.

10. Kapoor, Promilla : The Changing Status of Working Women in India, Vikas Publishing House, New Delhi, 1974, p. 56.

11. London School of Economics Report : Women, Wifc and Worker, 1970, p. 6.

12. Ranade and Ram Chandran : Women and Employment TISS study, 1970, p. 3.

13. Ramu, G. N. : Woman, Work and Marriage in Urban India, Sage Publisher, New Delhi/London, 1989, p. 59.

14. Sood, Rita : Changing Status and Adjustment of Women, Mahak Publishing Pvt Ltd, Jaipur, 1991, p. 91.

CHAPTER 4
INCIDENCE OF ROLE CONFLICT

The objective situation of the role conflict of the working women is primarily determined by her family situation. Family situation comprise of family size, number of children, availability of servants socio-economic status of the family

In this chapter an effort has been made to highlight the incidence of role conflict when working women find themselves in a great stress while doing two jobs - within and outside their homes. With different degrees of expectations from various members of their families such as husband, children, in-laws, guests, and on the other front from their employer, clients or patients and with the pressure of job they find themselves on a cross road of conflict.

Kapur, notes that additional roles of a working woman, to the set of her traditional roles of a wife and mother does create difficult situations and does produce conflict and tension within her on account of her desire to carry out her dual responsibilities of home and work efficiently. With multiplicity of roles, her behaviour becomes very confused in terms of 'expected' and actual conduct and she faces the major confusion with regards to her status and role.[1] (Ramu 1989 : 33)

Reaction of family members when the respondent is unable to attend to her family

Contingencies keep arising in day to day life and every one of us is required to face it. Family is an institution, where because of intimate emotional interaction a lot is expected from each other. When these expectations are not taken care of, especially during times of difficulty and emergency, it may lead to many types of conflicts. When the woman goes for work, her set of roles multiply many fold. But, does that also change the expectations of family members from her e.g., if there is a celebration at home or somebody, say the child/husband/in laws/parents is ill, does the family have same expectations from the working women as it would have from a non-working one. If the expectations are same irrespective of working or non-working status, there are bound to be conflicts regarding her multiple roles. She will not be able to devote her full time or take leave from work every now and then which will lead to conflicts at work place. It may also lead to a condition of stress and strain.

Table : 4.1 : Reaction of the family when unable to attend to family needs by their professing

Reaction of the family when unable to attend to family needs	Profession						
	Medicine	Law	Engineering	Teaching	Nursing	Social work	Total
Favourable	12.00 **90.00**	9.09 **35.00**	30.33 **70.00**	16.00 **80.00**	16.00 **45.00**	30.00 **60.00**	19.85 **63.33**
Unfavourable	10.00 **10.00**	9.09 **5.00**	14.00 **10.00**	6.00 -	18.00 **30.00**	12.00 -	11.76 **9.16**
Indifferent	2.00 -	- -	10.00 -	10.00 -	4.00 -	6.00 -	5.88 -
Understanding	74.00 -	81.82 **60.00**	46.00 **20.00**	62.00 **20.00**	62.00 **25.00**	44.00 **40.00**	59.56 **27.5**
Favourable and Understanding	2.00 -	- -	- -	6.00 -	- -	8.00 -	2.94 -
Total	100.00 **100.00**	100.00 **100.00**	100.00 **100.00**	100.00 **100.00**	100.00 **100.00**	100.00 **100.00**	100.00 **100.00**

The collected data show the following results :

It is clear from the table that professionals in small percentages only face unfavourable reaction from their family members whenever they are not able to attend to them properly because of their professional pursuit (11.76 and 9.16). The percentage further becomes low in the latter study reflecting more acceptance of a working women in the family.

In both the studies it is the nurses who face the unfavourable attitude in highest percentage (18.00 and 30.00) among the six professionals. Contrary to the percentage of other professionals facing unfavourable attitude, the percentage of nursing professionals in this category has gone up considerably, suggesting that the family of nursing professionals have become less receptive of their working status.

There has been a interchange in responses in the category favourable and understanding in the two studies; highest percent of professionals receive understanding attitude in 1990 and favourable attitude in 2002. Doctors get favourable attitude of their family members as largest percentages (90.00) amongst the six professions in 2002. While law professionals receive understanding attitude of the family members in largest percent (81.82) in 1990 study.

On the whole it can be said that the family members of the professionals show understanding and favourable attitude towards the professional who is not able to devote the required time or attention to them because of her working status and this stands true irrespective of the time gap between the two studies.

When unable to attend to the family by the type of the family

Another pertinent relationship which can be of interest and importance for this study is the reaction of the family members of the respondents when they come from joint and nuclear families. This will give an insight into the fact as to people in which kind of family have more expectations from the working professional.

A glance at the Table No 4.2 shows that in 1990, largest percent of respondents were from joint family receive understanding attitude (50.77) while in 2002 the attitude is favourable (69.09). In both the studies, the response remains positive. With regards to nuclear family also, the same trend is evident i.e. in 1990 understanding attitude is (67.61), and in 2002 favourable (58.46).

Interesting difference is observed when category of professionals receiving unfavourable attitude is studied. In 1990, it is the professionals from nuclear family who received unfavourable attitude in larger percent (15.49), while in 2002 it is the joint family professionals (10.90) who face unfavourable attitude of the family members. i.e. expectations in joint family have risen over a period of time.

Application of chi-square test on 1990 data show that the two variables are significantly associated (percentage of receiving unfavourable attitude from nuclear family is almost double of that from joint family) while in 2002, chi-square test show no significant association. Here joint family professional receiving unfavourable reaction are more in percentage while the difference between the two studies has narrowed down.

Table : 4.2 : When unable to attend to the family by the type of the family of the professional

Reaction of the family when unable to attend to them	TYPE OF FAMILY		
	Joint Family	Nuclear Family	Total
Favourable	30.00 **69.09**	10.50 **58.46**	19.85 **63.33**
Unfavourable	7.69 **10.90**	15.49 **7.69**	11.76 **9.16**
Understanding	50.77 **20.00**	67.61 **38.84**	59.56 **27.5**
Indifferent	7.69 -	4.23 -	5.88 -
Understanding and favourable	3.85 -	2.11 -	2.94 -
Total	47.79 **45.83**	52.21 **54.16**	100.00 **1.00**

X^2 (Cal) = 21.83; Tab = 9.49, $p < 0.05$ df = 4
X^2 = 29.45 df = 2 P > 0.05

Reaction of the family members by the religion

Religion in our country is seen as a guiding force for many causes of actions and behaviour. By studying this attribute (reaction of the family members when the respondent is not able to attend to her family properly) in relation to their religion, it can be ascertained that the professionals facing unfavourable reaction are coming from followers of which religion.

Table : 4.3 : Reaction of the family members by the religion of the professional

Reaction of the family	RELIGION					
	Hindu	Muslim	Siks	Christian	Jain	Total
Favourable	24.46 **55.67**	18.75 **100.00**	- **100.00**	17.14 **100.00**	14.29 **75.00**	19.85 **63.33**
Unfavourable	11.71 **10.30**	12.50 -	22.22 -	5.71 -	28.57 **25.00**	11.76 **9.16**
Understanding	59.51 **34.02**	50.00 -	44.44 -	68.57 -	57.14 -	59.56 **27.5**
Indifferent	6.34 -	6.25 -	- -	5.71 -	- -	5.88 -
Understanding & favourable	0.98 -	12.50 -	33.33 -	2.56 -	- -	2.94 -
Total	76.37 **80.83**	5.88 **7.5**	3.31 **3.33**	12.87 **5.00**	2.57 **3.33**	100.00 **100.00**

All the professionals from Muslim, Christian and Sikh communities receive favourable attitude of their family (100.00) while the Hindu professionals also receive the same response i.e. favourable (55.67) and understanding (34.02) in 2002. In 1990 also, respondents in general received these responses in large percentages. (favourable 19.85 and understanding 59.56)

Professionals receiving unfavourable response in both the studies belong to two communities that of Hindus (11.71 and 10.30), and Jains (28.57 and 25.0). But in the earlier study a small percent of respondents (5.88), did receive an indifferent attitude of the family, which may be potential source of conflict for the woman when she needs their cooperation. She is expected to shoulder some responsibility which she is unable to take up in wake of her working status, it may come up as a threat for conflict for her. Hindu (6.34), Muslim (6.25), and Christian (5.71) professionals reported of having faced the indifferent attitude.

Thus, irrespective of the change in mind-set of the society because of the rapid transformation of value systems (impact of western culture and values including more materialistic attitude of people in general), it is the Hindu and Jain professionals who face the antipathy and brunt of the family members, when they go out for discharging their professional responsibilities.

Attitude of people at home and reaction of the family members

Reaction of the family members when unable to attend to her family in wake of her employment and attitude of people at home towards her working professional status seems to be an important relationship to establish.

Table : 4.4 : Attitude of people at home toward the professional practice by the reaction of the family members

Attitude of people	Reaction of the family members			
	Favourable	**Unfavourable**	**Understanding**	**Total**
Favourable	92.59 **100.00**	50.00 **100.00**	87.64 **100.00**	81.62 **100.00**
Unfavourable	1.85 -	28.13 -	3.05 -	6.25 -
Indifferent	5.56 -	21.87 -	9.88 -	12.13 -
Total	19.85 **28.33**	11.77 **9.16**	62.50 **62.50**	100.00 **100.00**

When the two variables are matched, the overall picture which emerge out of the two studies remain the same.

Maximum percent of respondents in both studies reported to have an understanding reaction towards the professional, when she has not been able to attend to her family needs in wake of her employment. The percentage is same in both the studies i.e. 62.50%. But the significant difference lies in the fact that in the later study all the respondents (100.0) said that their family has a favourable attitude towards her employment whereas in the 1990 study 87.64% said that attitude of people at home is favourable where as 9.88% said that their family remains indifferent to their professional practice. While 3.05% of the respondents with understanding reaction profess that their family's attitude is unfavourable towards their profession, which seems to be quite paradoxical.

Amongst the respondents reporting favourable reaction (19.85 and 28.33) a great majority reported to be receiving favourable attitude also (92.50 and 100.00).

All the respondents in the latter study report to have favourable attitude of their family members toward their professional practice. All those respondents who said that they have to face unfavourable reaction when responsibility at home remains unfulfilled also get to see favourable attitude towards her working status. Only 9.16% of the respondents of the total sample in the latter study face unfavourable reaction which increases in 1990 (11.77) Here (1990), 28.13% of the respondents facing unfavourable reaction were subjected to unfavourable attitude towards her working outside the home.

On throwing light on the marital status of the respondents and the attitude of people at home towards the professional practice, we find in both the studies greater percent of respondents facing unfavourable attitude are from the married respondents (8.43 and 3.14) where as the separated (100.00 and 00.00) widows (100.00 and 90.70) receive the favourable attitude in large percentages.

Thus, it is seen that when the woman is widowed or separated, and is economically independent the family is in favour of her professional pursuit while the married women face unfavourable attitude to the maximum.

Professional practice affecting her family life

From every person in the society, there are some expectations which he/she has to fulfil. Family being a very close knit unit of the society, it becomes an important responsibility of every member to take care of his or her duties and responsibilities for smooth running of the institution. Women folk in the family form the core.

Traditionally, they have been assigned the task of taking care of the family members, especially their physical comforts. Apart from this, every member of the family also has a different set of expectations from the woman. As for example, the husband expects companionship, children her time, love and affection, brother, sister, in-laws, parents expect her to be helpful in fulfilling their daily needs related to house-hold chores. Thus the same women has to switch roles in the nick of time to appease each member in her family.

The working woman who is already busy due to the commitment to fulfil her job obligations, often finds herself in a great dilemma as to how to fulfil the varied kind of expectations at different walks of their life and this may create role conflict at times.

To assess the situation, a question related to the impact of pursuing their career on their family life was administered to the respondents. Following data have been gathered in this regard.

Fig : 4.5 : Effect on Family Life

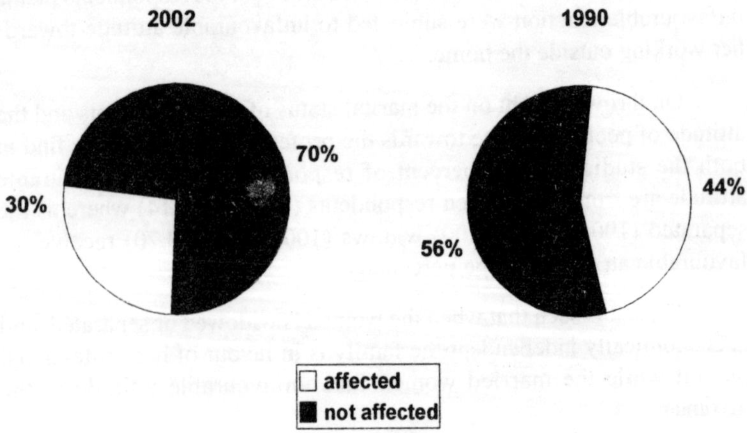

It is evident that respondents in large percentage feel that their professional practice does not affect their family life and the percentage has substantially increased. This reflects either better handling of the two fronts or reduced expectation from their kith and kin. In 1990 study no effect was reported in largest percent by teaching professionals (70.00), followed by social workers (62.00), and nursing professionals (60.00), while in 2002 study law professionals (95.00) reported no effect followed by nursing (90.00), and engineering professionals (80.00).

The category of professionals of 1990 study reporting no effect in large percentage, said in 2002 that it does effect their family life,- teaching (50.00) which is only next to medical professionals who in both the studies have lowest percent for no effect (46.00 and 40.00).

The study of collected data throws light on the fact that with passage of time, certain professionals (especially from teaching profession) have not been able to maintain a balance between the two fronts, thus effecting the expected family life of a woman. While other professionals like lawyers (45.45 and 95.00), and engineers (42.00 and 80.00) have been able to maintain a balance between professional demands and family life.

Increase in percentage of respondents speaking for the fact that the family life is not affected reflects on the general acceptance by the people at large about the working status of the woman, along with less of expectations from her as a wife, daughter, daughter-in-law, mother or in other roles.

Among those, whose family life is affected by their professional practice, maximum percentage is cited in the area of restricted social outings (23.16) in 1990, (maximum percentage from engineering (38.00)) and care of children in 2002 (14.16) (maximum percentage for doctors (40.00)). This reflects on two aspects – that, over a period of time expectations of socializations have come down, or that the working professional has equipped to maintain a better way to meet the socialization needs. Secondly, professionals in today's time have become more conscious about their responsibility towards their children.

Reference

1. Ramu, G.N: Women Worked and Marriage in Urban India. Sage Publication, New Delhi, (1989: p. 33).

CHAPTER 5
REFLECTORS OF ROLE CONFLICT

Any conflict gets reflected in the behaviour patterns and conduct of people who suffer from it. In case of role conflict also, the behaviour and conduct of women professionals reflect the inner conflict from which they suffer. It may be reflected in a variety of ways such as irritation, rough behaviour, etc. It is against this background that the reflection of role conflicts are being discussed here.

Attitude of people at home

Attitude of people about certain action or behaviour is governed by the degree of fulfillment of their aims and objectives in relations to that act or pattern of behaviour. If it takes care of their motives, attitude automatically becomes favourable. If it does not, it becomes unfavourable. We see another reaction, viz. being indifferent to the situation or person. When an individual does not feel involved in the situation, he/she may be displaying an attitude of indifference towards it. On incorporating the collected data in a tabular form, we find the following results :

Attitude and profession

The studies reveal that professionals in good majority enjoy favoruable attitude of their family members towards their pursuing the profession (81.62 and 98.33). The percentage has increased to all most 100% in the second study, reflecting the change in outlook of families in general towards women taking up their profession. It was learnt during the study that the family's attitude towards the professionals is so strongly positive that infant children of the respondents are being brought up by their in-laws, in a different city.

Table 5.1 Attitude of people at home by various variables

Profession	Attitude of people at home			Total
	Favourable	Unfavourable	Indifferent	
Medicine	86.00 **90.00**	6.00 **10.00**	8.00 -	100.00 **100.00**
Law	90.91 **100.00**	- -	9.09 -	100.00 **100.00**
Engineering	72.00 **100.00**	10.00 -	18.00 -	100.00 **100.00**
Teaching	92.00 **100.00**	2.00 -	6.00 -	100.00 **100.00**
Nursing	72.00 **100.00**	10.00 -	18.00 -	100.00 **100.00**
Social Work	82.00 **100.00**	6.00 -	12.00 -	100.00 **100.00**
Total	81.62 **98.33**	6.75 **1.66**	12.13 -	100.00 **100.00**
Religion				
Hindu	83.90 **97.93**	5.37 **2.07**	10.73 -	100.00 **100.00**
Muslim	68.75 **100.00**	12.50 -	18.75 -	100.00 **100.00**
Christian	77.14 **100.00**	5.72 -	17.14 -	100.00 **100.00**
Sikh	77.78 **100.00**	22.22 -	 -	100.00 **100.00**
Jain	71.43 **100.00**	 -	28.57 -	100.00 **100.00**
Caste				
Brahmin	83.64 **100.00**	5.45 -	10.91 -	100.00 **100.00**
Vaishya	77.42 **100.00**	16.13 -	6.45 -	100.00 **100.00**
Rajput	76.0 **100.00**	4.00 -	20.00 -	100.00 **100.00**
Khatri	76.0 **100.00**	8.00 -	16.00 -	100.00 **100.00**
Kayastha	86.44 **92.30**	1.69 **7.70**	11.87 -	100.00 **100.00**
SC & OBC	100.00 **100.00**	- -	- -	100.00 **100.00**

No. of children

No Children	84.62 **100.00**	7.69 -	7.69 -	100.00 **100.00**
One Child	65.22 **89.47**	10.87 **10.53**	23.91 -	100.00 **100.00**
2-3 Children	82.48 **100.00**	4.12 -	13.40 -	100.00 **100.00**
More than 3 children	66.67 **100.00**	9.52 -	23.81 -	100.00 **100.00**
		6.90	15.76	100.00

X^2 (cal) = 10.75, tab = 12.59, p> 0.05, df=6
X^2 = 5.844 , df=3 p>0.05

Age group of children

Upto 2 yrs.	68.12 **100.00**	15.79 -	15.79 -	100.00 **100.00**
3-6 yrs.	69.23 **85.71**	7.69 **14.29**	23.08 -	100.00 **100.00**
7-14 yrs.	82.43 **100.00**	4.06	13.51 -	100.00 **100.00**
More than 14 yrs.	85.94 **100.00**	3.12 -	10.97 -	100.00 **100.00**

X^2 (cal) = 9.76, tab = 12.59, p> 0.05, df=6
X^2 = 9.814 , df=3 p<0.05

Period of service

Just joined	70.00 **100.00**	10.00 -	20.00 -	100.00 **100.00**
Less than a year	92.31 **100.00**	- -	7.69 -	100.00 **100.00**
Between 1-3 Year	100.0 **100.00**	- -	- -	100.00 **100.00**
Between 3-5 Year	80.00 **100.00**	8.00 -	12.00 -	100.00 **100.00**
More than 5 year	78.97 **97.05**	7.18 **2.95**	13.85 -	100.00 **100.00**

Degree of interest

Very keen	93.55 **100.00**	2.15 -	4.30 -	100.00 **100.00**
Keen	85.22 **100.00**	3.48 -	11.30 -	100.00 **100.00**
In different	59.65 **100.00**	14.04 -	26.31 -	100.00 **100.00**
Not helpful	42.86 **93.33**	42.86 **6.66**	14.28 -	100.00 **100.00**

Specific behaviour shown by the family members

Provided a congenial atmosphere for work	90.70 **100.00**	1.86 -	7.44 -	100.00 **100.00**
Don't bother about my going out of the family	53.33 **71.42**	15.56 **28.57**	31.11 -	100.00 **100.00**
Pass sarcastic comments and harass	25.00 -	50.00 -	25.00 -	100.00 -

X^2 (cal) = 76.85, (Tab) = 9.49, $p< 0.05$, df=4
X^2 = 17.714, df=1, $p<0.05$

In 2002 study, only one professiòn has respondents saying that they face unfavourable attitude of their family, the profession being that of medicine (10.00), whereas in the earlier study it was the professionals from engineering (10.00) and nursing (10.00) professions. The total percentage of respondents facing unfavorable attitude has also lowered to 1.66% (in 2002) from 6.75% (in 1990). Thus it can be said that attitude of people at home towards the practice of the profession has become more acceptable irrespective of the profession she is in.

In 2002 study, unfavourable attitude of the family is faced by only Hindu professionals (2.07) from Kayastha's community (7.70) having one child (10.53) in the age group of 3-6 yrs (14.29). These professionals have been in the service for more than 5 years (2.95).

Schedule caste and OBC professionals receive favourable attitude by 100.00% in both the studies Clearly, the families of SC and OBC professionals have been taking the professional practice of their women folk very positively and encouragingly.

The other highlights of 1990 study are teaching (92.00), followed by law (90.00) professionals, mostly Hindus (83.90) from Kayasthas community (86.44), followed by Brahmins (83.64 caste) with no children (84.62) and working between 1-3 yrs. received favourable attitude of the family in largest percentages. People at home showed very keen interest in promotion of their career (93.55) and they were provided with congenial atmosphere at home for taking up her professional pursuit.

While engineering (10.00) and nursing (10.00) professionals from Sikh (22.22) and Muslim (12.50) community; Vaishyas among Hindus (16.13) having one child (10.87), or having more than 3 children (9.52) from the age group of 0-2 yrs, and who have just joined their service, face unhelpful attitude (42.86) towards the degree of promotion of their career and listened to sarcastic comments (50.00) of their family members faced unfavourable attitude of the family members in largest percentages.

Incidents of professionals facing indifferent attitude of the family towards the professional practice was also observed in 1990 study (12.13). This category does not exist in 2002 study. Indifferent attitude is represented by engineers and nurses (18.00 each), Muslims (18.75), Rajputs amongst Hindus (20.00) with one child (23.91); or more than 3 children (23.81), in the age group of 2-6 years (23.08) and had just joined their service (20.00) were in largest percentages.

To conclude, it can be said that the empirical data in the fore running tables show that the professionals, irrespective of the profession they are in, the religion they follow, the caste to which they belong, the number of children they have and their age group, period of service they have put in for the profession, degree of interest shown by the family in promotion of her career, and specific behaviour of the family members receive favoruable attitude towards their professional practice.

On application of chi-square test on 2002 data, significant relationship with attitude of people at home towards the professional pursuit emerge with attributes like age-group of children, and specific behaviour shown by the family members to reflect their degree of interest. On applying the same test on 1990 data significant relationship emerge only with specific behaviour shown to prove the same.

Extent of help provided to the professionals

The extent to which the working professionals get help from their family members, will determine the extent to which her conflicts arising out of her responsibilities at home can be assessed.

When analyzed in the light of the extent of help she gets from her family in shouldering her house hold responsibilities, the picture that emerge in both the studies, is that a large percentage of professionals get much help in sharing of her work at home (57.7 and 45.83). The profession wise break up runs as – medicine (46.00 and 50.00), law (63.63 ad 60.00), engineering (74.00 and 15.00), teaching (46.00 and 70.00), nursing (52.00 and 30.00), and social work (68.00 and 50.00).

Teaching professionals are getting more help now and percentage of engineering professionals getting much help has become much less. Professionals who say that they receive only little help at home are engineers (60.00 in 2002); doctors (38.00) and teachers (36.00) in the 1990 study. The percentage of professionals receiving no help has reduced from 19.85% of the total sample in 1990 to 15.83% of the total sample in 2002.

Nurses (32.00 and 30.00) in 1990 receive no help, show highest percentages in both the studies, while 30.00% of the social workers in 2002 also receive no help in their domestic work from their family members.

On 1990 data, chi-square test show that calculated value is 28.06, while the tabulated value is 18.31 when degree of freedom is 10, and probability is <0.05 suggesting, that the attributes have a positive association. The same test when applied on 2002 data show the value of chi-square as 77.15 when the df=15 and probability is less than 0.05. Infact, the relationship is highly associated as the value of P is 0.000000448.

Extent of help and type of family

When the variable of extent of help provided by the family members in doing her house hold work was seen in light of type of family the professional comes from, the following trend emerge :

Table 5.2 Extent of help provided by the family members by the type of family

Help Given	Joint Family	Nuclear Family	Total
Much Help	71.54 **69.09**	45.07 **26.15**	57.72 **45.83**
Little Help	17.69 **29.04**	26.76 **33.84**	22.43 **31.66**
No Help	10.77 **1.8**	28.17 **33.86**	19.85 **6.66**
Not Applicable	- -	- **12.30**	- **15.83**
Total	100.00 **100.00**	100.00 **100.00**	100.00 **100.00**

X^2 (cal) = 21.13, (tab) = 3.99, $p < 0.05$, df=2

X^2 = 31.56, df=3 $p<0.05$

The data very clearly shows that in both the studies, professionals coming from joint family get much help in very high percentages (71.54 and 69.09), while professionals from nuclear family receive much help in case of only 45.07% professionals in 1990, which has further reduced to 26.15% in 2002.

The reason why the professionals still prefer to live in a joint family system is probably because of the fact that their family responsibilities get shared among the members than when they live in nuclear set up.

Professionals receiving no help from the family in sharing of domestic chores is also high amongst those who are in nuclear family 33.86% in 2002, and 26.76% in 1990; whereas, in joint family only small percentage of professional profess to get no help (10.77 and 1.80).

Both the studies suggest that the joint family set up is helpful in sharing the domestic responsibilities of the working professionals.

Application of chi-square test also suggests that the two attributes of extent of help and type of family are highly significant to each other. This result is same for both the studies.

Degree of Interest of the family members in promotion of their career.

Table 5.3: Degree of interest in relation to other variables

Profession

	Degree of Interest					
	Very Keen	**Keen**	**Indifferent**	**Unhelpful**	**Not helpful**	**Total**
Medicine	36.00	42.00	20.00	2.00	-	100.00
	50.00	**10.00**	**10.00**	-	**30.00**	**100.00**
Law	54.55	36.36	9.09	-	-	100.00
	20.00	**70.00**	**5.00**	-	**5.00**	**100.00**
Engineering	26.00	54.00	18.00	2.00	-	100.00
	-	**85.00**	-	-	**15.00**	**100.00**
Teaching	42.00	42.00	16.00	-	-	100.00
	10.00	**40.00**	-	-	**50.00**	**100.00**
Nursing	26.00	42.00	26.00	6.00	-	100.00
	10.00	**70.00**	-	-	**20.00**	**100.00**
Social Work	32.00	34.00	30.00	4.00	-	100.00
	20.00	**50.00**	-	-	**30.00**	**100.00**

X^2 (cal) = 15.09, tabulated = 18.31, $p > 0.05$, df=15
X^2 = 46.15, df=15, $p < 0.05$

Religion of the Professional

	Degree of Interest					
	Very Keen	**Keen**	**Indifferent**	**Unhelpful**	**Not helpful**	**Total**
Hindu	37.07	40.00	20.49	2.43	-	100.00
	16.49	**58.76**	**3.09**	-	**21.64**	**100.00**
Muslim	43.75	31.25	25.00		-	100.00
	44.44	**22.22**	-	-	**33.33**	**100.00**
Sikh		77.78	22.22	-	-	100.00
	50.00	**35.00**	-	-	**15.00**	**100.00**
Christian	20.00	51.43	22.86	5.71	-	100.00
	-	**100.00**	-	-	-	**100.00**
Jain	42.86	42.86	14.28		-	100.00
	-	-	-	-	**100.00**	**100.00**

Caste of Hindu Professionals

Brahmin	23.64 **13.79**	30.91 **62.06**	41.82 **-**	3.63 **-**	- **24.13**	100.00 **100.00**
Vaishya	45.16 **17.64**	38.71 **52.94**	16.13 **5.88**	- **-**	- **23.52**	100.00 **100.00**
Rajput	32.00 **60.00**	52.00 **40.00**	16.00 **-**	- **-**	- **-**	100.00 **100.00**
Khatri	48.00 **-**	28.00 **75.00**	16.00 **-**	8.00 **-**	 **25.00**	100.00 **100.00**
Kayashta	40.68 **19.23**	47.46 **50.00**	10.17 **7.69**	1.69 **-**	- **23.07**	100.00 **100.00**
SC/OBC	50.00 **8.3**	50.00 **75.00**	- **-**	- **-**	- **16.60**	100.00 **100.00**
Total	34.19 **18.33**	42.28 **54.12**	20.96 **2.50**	2.57 **-**	- **25.00**	100.00 **100.00**

Degree of interest and profession

After studying the extent of help provided to the professional, next thing which comes to mind is the degree of interest the family show in promotion of her career. If the family also takes interest in professional's scaling new achievements in her career, morale of the woman gets accentuated. Then, she becomes more careful that because of her professional demands, she has not to overlook her family members in any respect – their physical comforts, mental, psychological and emotional needs, and does not mind doling out her salary on the family expenses.

The empirical data when seen in relation to the profession, show that the largest percentage of professionals say that their family is 'keen' about promotion of their career (42.28 and 54.12). In 1990 study, the percentages are evenly dispersed, between 34.50% to 54.00% amongst the six professions while in 2002 study, except for medicine (10.00 only) other professions show quite high percentages between 40.00% (teaching) to 85.00% (engineering). Highest percentage of professional coming out with opinion very keen interest of their family in promotion of their career come form Medicine (50.00) in 2002 and law (54.55) in 1990.

In 2002, 25.00% of the professionals say that their family is neither helpful nor unhelpful towards their career. It was explained like this, that the family members neither create any hassles in pursuing the professional practice nor they show any special interest in promotion of their career.

They are neither indifferent or apathetic towards the issue, nor are they helpful, as explained by professionals. And, some of the professions have a sizeable percentage of professionals speaking out this option -- teaching (50.00), medicine and social work (30.00 each,) nursing (20.00) and engineering (15.00) and law (5.00). Infact this category has professionals from all the six professionals. This may reflect on the fact that the family has accepted, even if unwillingly, that when the woman in the family is professionally qualified, by virtue of her training/ qualification she will pursue her career.

In 1990 study, the professionals from all the six professions, said that their family showed indifference towards their career (20.96), while unhelpful attitude and behaviour was also reported by 2.57% professionals, from nursing (6.00), social work (4.00), and medicine and engineering (2.00 each).

Application of X^2 test on 1990, show that the two variables have no association while, the same test when applied on 2002 data, shows that the two variables have very high degree of association (p=0.000049)

Degree of interest by Religion

This is to assess what role the religion has to play in showing the degree of interest in promotion of the career of the professionals. In both the studies, Hindu professional, in maximum percentages, said that their family show keen interest (40.00 and 58.76), while very keen interest is received by 37.07% hindu respondents in 1990 and 16.49% in 2002 study. 2.43% Hindu professionals face unhelpful attitude (1990), and 21.64% Hindu professionals report of not helpful attitude (2002).

Amongst the Muslim respondent, largest percentages come from the category of very keen interest (43.75 and 44.44), while keen category has 31.25%, in 1990 and 22.22% professionals in 2002. The study conducted in 2002 also show that 33.33% Muslim professionals saying not helpful attitude of their family.

In 2002 Sikhs professionals receive very keen interest (50.00) in largest percentage while they received keen interest (77.82) in earlier study. Christain respondents (51.43and 100.00) in majority say that they find their family to be keen about their professional achievements.

In 1990 Jain respondents in majority faced a positive response but in 2002 all of then face not-helpful attitude towards their professional career. Unhelpful attitude is faced by only Hindu (2.43) and Christian (5.71) professionals in 1990.

Degree of Interest and Caste

This is to study the impact of caste of the Hindu respondent, on the degree of promotion of her career. Amongst the Brahmins, the largest percentage of professionals faced indifferent attitude (41.82) in 1990, while in 2002, the family show keen interest (62.06).

Vaishya professionals reported of very keen interest (45.16), in the 1990 study, and keen interest (52.94) in 2002 study; Rajputs–keen (52.00) in 1990, and very keen (60.00) in 2002; Khatri–very keen interest (48.00), and keen interest (75.00) in 2002. Amongst Kayastha, in both the studies, professionals in largest percentages report of keen interest (47.46 and 50.00).

While SC/ OBC professionals received very keen and keen interest in equal percentages (50.00 and 50.00) in 1990. In 2002, majority i.e. 75.00% of these SC/OBC professionals report of their family showing keen interest.

Unhelpful attitude is shown by the family of professionals from Brahmins (3.63), Khatris (8.40) and Kayashtas (1.69) in 1990, while in 2002, Brahmins (24.13), Viashya (23.52), Khartis (25.00), Kayasthas (23.00), and SC/ OBC (16.66) report of their family showing not helpful attitude towards the promotion of their career.

Thus, it can be concluded that professionals in both the studies irrespective of their caste generally get positive attitude towards the promotion of their career. While in small percentages women receive unhelpful behaviour in 1990 and not helpful attitude in little higher percentages in 2002.

If not working, relationship with other people at home (other than the husband)

This is to get a preview into a situation that if she was not a working woman and spends all her time at home like any other housewife, then what does the professional think would have been her relationship with other people at home. Other people in this context include relatives and children (in case of nuclear family), in-laws and other relations (in case of married professionals living in joint family), parents, brother and sister (in case of unmarried professional).

Table 5.4 Possible relationship by the profession

Possible relationship	Medicine	Law	Engineering	Teaching	Nursing	Social work	Total
Same	52.00 **25.00**	50.00 **50.00**	50.00 **30.00**	58.00 **50.00**	25.00 **70.00**	56.00 **35.00**	48.44 **43.33**
Can't Say	20.00	30.00	10.00	22.92 **10.00**	8.33	14.00 **15.00**	16.41 **4.16**
Different	28.00 **75.00**	20.00 **50.00**	40.00 **70.00**	18.75 **40.00**	66.67 **30.00**	30.00 **50.00**	35.15 **52.5**
Total	100.00 **100.00**	100.00 **100.00**	100.00 **100.00**	100.00 **100.00**	100.00 **100.00**	100.00 **100.00**	100.00 **100.00**

In 1990 study largest percent of respondents said that their relationships with their family members will remain the same (48.44) irrespective of their working or non working status. While in 2002 the largest percentage is of those professionals who say that their relationship would have been different (52.15); doctors (75.00) and engineers (70.00) held this opinion in great majority.

A sizeable percent (16.4) of respondents in 1990 said that they can't say what would be the possibility; the percent of respondent became very small in 2002 (4.16), showing that professionals are able to make better assessment of the situation whether it will improve or deteriorate or will remain the same.

In 1990, nurses (66.67) were the only professionals who in large percent, said that their relationship would have been different, if not working. While in 2002 it is again the nurses who professed in largest percentage that the relationship will remain the same (70.00).

Different	**More Cordial**	41.11 **45.66**
	More Strained	58.89 **54.65**

When different relationship is reported by the professionals 41.11% in 1990 and 45.66% in 2002, say that they will have more cordial relationship because these women will give more time and attention to their family. Social workers in both the studies professed that in high percentages (60.00 and 58.33 of those who said of different relationship) followed by engineers (50.00 and 66.66), doctors (42.86 and 50.00).

It can be concluded that these professions are more demanding, especially in terms of time devoted to it, have more professionals feeling that their non working status will lead to giving more time and attention to their family members.

More strained relationship is reported in majority by 58.89% in 1990, and 54.65% in 2002. The reason for this strained relationship in 2002 was lack of professional satisfaction leading to frustration (42.62), and in 1990, no financial help to the family (37.74), followed by more time for confrontation at home (33.96).

At the time of the earlier study, the financial aspects of working were prominent, which was reflected in the reason for taking up of professional practice. While in the recent study it is the professional satisfaction which has become more important aspect of professional pursuit.

If not-working, type of relationship with their husband

In the previous table we have studied the type of relationship with other people at home which the professional assess in case of their non working status. The husband plays an important role in the life of a married woman in India, as the women here are largely dependent on him emotionally, psychologically as well as financially. In the course of these studies, even if we rule out financial dependence, other factors (emotional and psychological) hold true. The pivotal role played by the husband in Indian society cannot be overlooked. In this contest, it becomes very important to find out what would have been the type of relationship of the professionals with their husband, if they wouldn't have been working.

Table : 5.5: Possible type of relationship with the husband if not working by the profession

Possible type of relationship	Profession						
	Medicine	Law	Engineer-ing	Teaching	Nursing	Social Work	Total
Same	45.00 **28.57**	57.14 **60.00**	44.12 **28.57**	50.00 **62.5**	27.27 **100.00**	82.76 **50.00**	49.44 **43.93**
Can't Say	30.00 -	14.28 -	8.82 -	25.00 **12.5**	18.18 -	- -	16.85 **1.51**
Different	25.00 **71.42**	28.57 **40.00**	47.06 **71.43**	25.00 **25.00**	54.55 -	17.24 **50.00**	33.71 **54.54**
Total	100.00 **100.00**	100.00 **100.00**	100.00 **100.00**	100.00 **100.00**	100.00 **100.00**	100.00 **100.00**	100.00 **100.00**

Different → **More Cordial** 40.00 **25.00**

Different → **More Strained** 60.00 **75.00**

The empirical data of the two studies shows that the largest percentage of professionals in 1990 were of the opinion that their relationship with their husband would have been same (49.44), with the highest percentage coming from the profession of social work (82.76). In 2002 all the nursing professionals say that their relationship will remain the same, irrespective of their working or non-working status.

Professionals in more percentages in 2002 have opined of having different relationship with their husband (54.54) – 25.00% of them saying it will be more cordial, while 75.00% are of view that it will be more strained. Frustration on the part of the professional for not being able to work, was given the reason by maximum percent of women in 2002. Medicine (100.00) and teaching profession (100.00) said it in highest percents. While in 1990, strained relationship because of no financial help was the reason given by majority. Law (100.00) and nursing (76.92) said it in highest percentages.

It is observed here, as in the case of relationship with other people in the family, with respect to the change in relationship, especially when strained is opted for, it's the professional satisfaction which matters in 2002 study, while in 1990, it's the finances generated by pursuing the profession which played an important or governing role.

Possible relationship if not working by the type of family

In the preceeding paragraph, we have studied the possible type of relationship of the professionals with their husband and other people at home, in relation to their profession. But the impact of the type of family from which the professional come from has a significant role in establishing the association between the two variables

Table : 5.6: Possible type of relationship if not working, by the type of family

a) With other people at home (other than the husband)

Possible relationship	Type of family		
	Joint	Nuclear	Total
Same	51.63 **43.63**	43.69 **44.61**	48.44 **44.16**
Can't say	15.69 **-**	17.48 **6.15**	16.40 **3.33**
Different	32.68 **56.37**	38.83 **49.24**	35.16 **52.67**
Total	100.00 **100.00**	100.00 **100.00**	100.00 **100.00**

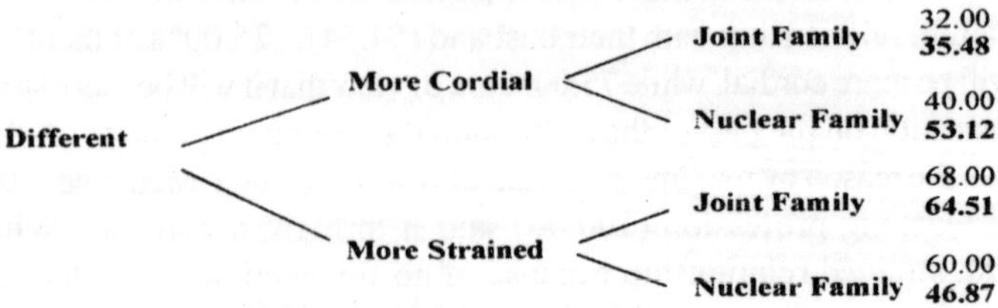

X^2(cal)= 2.23; (Tab)= 7.81 $p > 0.05$ df = 2

$X^2 = 3.680$ df = 2 $p > 0.05$

b) With the husband (in case of married respondents)

Possible relationship	Type of family		
	Joint	**Nuclear**	**Total**
Same	52.27 **38.09**	45.65 **48.88**	48.89 **45.44**
Can't say	18.18 **4.76**	15.22 -	16.67 **1.51**
Different	29.55 **57.14**	39.13 **51.11**	34.34 **53.03**
Total	100.00 **100.00**	100.00 **100.00**	100.00 **100.00**

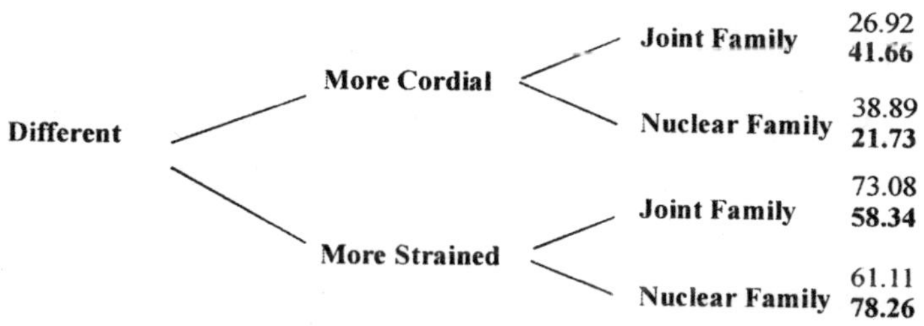

X^2(cal)= 2.78; (Tab)= 7.81 p >0.05 df = 2

X^2 = 2.608 df = 2 p> 0.05

The comparisons of the collected data from both the studies show that in 1990 with 48.44% of respondent's it was same relationship with other people which was reported in highest percent, and in 2002, at 52.67% it is different relationship which has been reported by majority. There seems to be no relationship between the possible type of relationship if not working and the type of family she came from.

In 1990, when the professional opted for same, both joint (51.63) and nuclear (43.69) family professionals were in larger percentage. The data in both the studies show that professionals have more percentage in more cordial relationship in nuclear family than from joint family set up. Other people relate to children in the nuclear family, and by being at home the children's care and attention will be more. When in joint family, the professional may be with her in-laws or her parents, where there are more expectations from the woman; whether financial or sharing of household work and there are chances of confrontation in the family. Thus, female coming from joint family, in large percents have expressed more strained relationship (68.00 and 64.51). Application of chi-square test on both the data also doesn't support any association between the two attributes.

When the same attributes were studied with regards to the relationship with the husband in case of married respondents, the same trend was seen here also. Relationship remaining same was opined in largest percentage in 1990 (joint – 52.27, and nuclear 45.65) and different relationship in 2002 (joint- 57. 14, and nuclear 51.11). When the data was compared among professionals with opinion different both the studies reflect on more strained relationship irrespective of the type of family.

Most of the professionals said it was the frustration of sitting at home which leads to a more strained relationship with their husband.

When X^2 test was applied to both the data, it was found that the two variables bear no significant relationship, in both instances. The finding is concurring with the results of empirical data analysis.

Possible type of relationship and religion

In Indian society religion has profound impact on the values a person possess. If any act or practice does not have the approval of the religious beliefs, it is looked down upon in our Indian society. Some religions have rigid women customs, which prevail in society inspite of the class, educational status or any other distinguished attainment of an individual. In this study, the women are well educated and have a mind and opinion of their own.

In such a situation, how does religion affect the woman, who is qualified to take up a profession but supposedly has not take it up. This becomes an important aspect to assess, both with regard to people at home, and the husband in particular.

Table : 5.7 : Possible relationship if not working, by the religion

a) with other people at home (other than the husband)

Possible Relationship	Religion					
	Hindu	Muslim	Sikh	Christian	Jain	Total
Same	51.56 **40.20**	50.00 -	25.00 **30.00**	34.29 **66.66**	60.00 -	48.44 **37.5**
Can't say	15.63 **2.06**	18.75 **22.22**	12.50 -	20.00 -	20.00 -	16.40 **3.33**
Different	32.81 **57.74**	31.25 **77.78**	62.50 **70.00**	45.71 **33.33**	20.00 **100.00**	35.16 **69.16**
More Cordial	39.68 **50.00**	80.00 **28.57**	40.00 -	12.50 -	 -	36.37 **42.15**
More Strained	60.32 **50.00**	20.00 **71.42**	60.00 **100.00**	87.50 **100.00**	100.00 **100.00**	63.33 **57.74**

b) with the husband in case of married professional

Possible Relationship	Religion					
	Hindu	Muslim	Sikh	Christian	Jain	Total
Same	54.07 **45.28**	54.55 -	28.57 **100.00**	22.73 **100.00**	40.00 -	48.89 **42.42**
Can't say	14.82	18.18 **33.33**	-	31.82 -	20.00 -	16.67 **3.03**
Different	31.11 **54.71**	27.27 **66.66**	71.43 -	44.45 -	40.00 **100.00**	34.44 **54.54**
More Cordial	42.86 **31.03**	66.67 -	60.00 -	10.00 -	100.00 -	41.94 **25.00**
More Strained	57.14 **68.97**	33.33 **100.00**	40.00 -	90.00 -	- **100.00**	58.06 **75.00**

The analysis of data of both the studies reveal that in 1990, same relationship with other people at home was reported by Jains (60.00) Hindus (51.56) and Muslims (50.00) in large percentage.

While in 2002, only Christian professionals opined to have same relationship (66.66), in large percentage. In 2002, except for Christian respondents all the other professionals in high percentage report of different relationship. Among respondents opining different relationship, except for Hindu respondents, women from other religions in last percentages profess to have had a strained relationship. While in 1990, except for Muslim women, others reported of different and more strained relationship.

Thus, on comparing the two studies, when the respondents reported different relationship, professionals in more percentage say that they would have more strained relationship with people at home which is true for both studies.

When the attributes are studied in relation to the husband, it was found that 'same relationship' appear in more percent in 1990. All Sikh and Christian professionals in 2002 professed to have the same relationship, while in 1990, it was the Muslim professional (54.55) and the Hindu (54.09) who had the highest percentages.

All the Jain professionals (100.00) said to having different relationship in 2002, while in 1990 it was the Sikh professionals (71.43) who said it in highest percentage. In 1990, Muslim (66.67) and Jain (100.00) professionals said to be having a more cordial relationship with their husband if not working, but in 2002 study, the working women from the same religion said that their relationship will be more strained, both Muslim (100.00) and Jain (100.00).

It can be concluded that in 1990, it was the Jain and the Muslim women who would have had a more cordial relationship with their husband, if not working. Whereas in 2002, except for Hindu respondent in small percentage, respondent in no other religion would have experienced a more cordial and warm relationship. The 2002 study suggests, if not same, then it would have been strained or deteriorated relationship in the cases of majority of Hindu, all Muslim and Jain professionals.

Change in home environment

This is to enquire what changes the working professionals would like to have in their home environment so as to facilitate better co-ordination between home and work place. Change in home environment would be subtle reflection on areas of conflict or stress, which the professionals would like to be taken care of.

Both the studies have 60.00% of the professionals reporting that they don't need any change in their home environment so as to smoothen their working at the two fronts. This clearly indicates that they are quite satisfied with the environment and the facilities available to them at home, thus minimising the chances to reduce the conflict stress, or being over burdened both emotionally and physically.

Among those who wanted some change; better servants (28.97) was a change demanded in 1990, and more cooperation from the family members (58.33) in 2002. Doctors (24.00) and engineers (14.00) were in highest percents in 1990, calling for better servants. Engineers (100.00) and nurses (100.00) want more cooperation from their family in 2002 study.

Other changes asked for, in small percentages, in both the studies are, pleasant atmosphere at home (19.62 and 10.41), presence of an elder person (like grand mother) at home (7.47 and 2.08), and more cooperation at home (7.47 and 2.08).

Change in work environment

It becomes equally important to find out what changes these women want in their work environment or facilities at the place of work, so that working at both places become more convenient and tension free.

Only 29.41% in 1990, and 21.66% women in 2002 say that they don't want any change in the environment of their work place. Women in large percentage look forward to change in their work environment. We have seen earlier that while a different scenario emerges when the question of change in home environment is raised. In both the studies, greater percentage of women asked for some or the other change (70.59 and 78.33) at work front.

More cooperation from the people at work place has been asked for in large percentages, in both the studies (16.91 and 28.72), with the highest percent coming from the profession of medicine (26.00) and nursing (26.00) in 1990, and in 2002, from engineering (55.00), law (35.00) and medicine (40.00).

Other changes desired in 1990 were adequate staff, equipment and funds (19.85)–nurses (48.00) and doctors (34.00) said it in high percents; working hours to be reduced (25.00)–engineering professionals (58.00) and social work (24.00); better administration and discipline [nursing (16.00), social work (14.00) and engineering (12.00)].

In 2002, changes desired for are change in infrastructure (10.63), fast promotions (15.95) protested by 25.00% of engineers and 20.00% of teachers; more resources and autonomy in work (12.76) advocated by 30.00% nurses, 20.00% social workers; decentralization of responsibilities is desired by 6.38% respondents – engineers (10.00) and social workers (10.00).

Profession specific changes were—less corruption (law, in both studies), less work load and tension (teaching, 1990), campus residence (doctors and nurses, 1990), more holidays (engineering, 1990), night duty for 8 hours only (nurses, 1990), increase in salary (teachers, 1990), cultured atmosphere (doctors and engineers in1990).

Thus we see that the professionals have come out with various suggestions and demands for changes and facilities which they want to have at the work place, to reduce their stress and help in reducing conflicts.

When required to stay beyond prescribed hours of working

At times a situation arises when the working woman has to stay back at the place of work, after the prescribed working hours. This situation may arise because of work pressure, or stretching over of work already in process, which cannot be left for the next day. In such a situation, the women is caught in a dilemma. If she leaves the work incomplete, she has to face the consequences as a professional. And, if she doesn't reach home in time, people at home get offended. Often an unpleasant situation arises.

Table : 5.8 (a) : Measures adopted, when required to stay back by the profession

Measures adopted	Profession						
	Medicine	Law	Engineer-ing	Teaching	Nursing	Social work	Total
Inform at home	90.00 **70.00**	81.82 **85.00**	46.00 **100.00**	64.00 **85.00**	26.00 **30.00**	78.00 **80.00**	62.50 **75.00**
Want to inform but unable to do so	8.00 -	9.09 -	6.00 -	18.00 -	44.00 -	16.00 -	17.65 -
No need to inform	2.00 **30.00**	9.09 **15.00**	2.00 -	18.00 **15.00**	30.00	6.00 **20.00**	11.40 **13.33**
Not required to stay back	- -	- -	46.00 -	- -	- **70.00**	- -	8.45 **5.83**

Table : 5.8 (b) : Reaction of the family when unable to inform, by their profession

Get worried	59.93 **82.22**	Come to enquire	10.62 **6.66**
Get angry	14.04 **4.44**	They don't require	15.44 **6.66**

Large percentages of professionals report that they inform at home, when required to over stay at the place of work (62.50 and 75.00). In both the studies, large percentages can be seen in this category from all the professions, except in nursing. (wheres in 2002 a large number say that they are not required to over stay). While in 1990, the nurses in good percent said that they want to inform but are not able to do so (44.00). Another reaction of the nursing professionals, had been that there is no need to inform (30.00).

On enquiring about the reaction of the family members when they are not informed, respondents in very large numbers said that people at home get worried (59.93 and 82.22). The next category is that of the professionals, who feel that then family doesnot need to be informed (11.40 and 13.33). Doctors (30.00) said this in largest percent in 2002, while in 1990 nurses (30.00) and teachers (18.00) said this in the largest percent.

Family members get angry (14.04 and 4.44) and even come to enquire about the reason for delay (10.62 and 6.66).

Change in behaviour after unpleasantness at home

If there is some unpleasantness at home, the unpleasant mood is bound to be carried over to the place of work. Because of close interaction among the family members, there are always chances of some unpleasant episode or altercation. It may be because of children, husband, brother, sister or even parents. Such, interaction at times, when serious is nature, leaves its impression on the affected person, spoiling her mood and hampering her performance both at home and work place.

The impact may be reflected on the various roles the woman has to play and conflicts which may arise out of it, especially when she has to switch from one set of roles to another different set of roles.

The empirical data show that in 1990, 53.68% respondents said that there is no change in their behaviour, whereas in 2002, only 45.00% opined this. The lowering of percentage show that the women have become more open about expressing their state of mind to people around them. Lawyers (72.73) in 1990, and Nurses (70.00) in 2002 hold 'no change' opinion in largest percentage.

Table : 5.9 : Change in behaviour by the profession

Change in behaviour	Profession						
	Medicine	**Law**	**Engineer-ing**	**Teaching**	**Nursing**	**Social work**	**Total**
Become quiet and	8.00	4.00	20.00	6.00	18.00	8.00	11.76
depressed	**5.00**	**5.00**	-	**10.00**	**20.00**	**30.00**	**11.00**
Cannot concentrate/	2.00	4.00	6.00	2.00	2.00	12.00	5.14
gets distracted	**5.00**	-	-	**20.00**	-	-	**4.16**
Tensed/stressed	16.00	-	8.00	8.00	4.00	20.00	10.29
	40.00	**25.00**	**35.00**	-	-	**10.00**	**18.33**
Get irritated/angry	30.00	4.00	22.00	20.00	-	14.00	18.38
	10.00	**10.00**	-	**10.00**	**10.00**	**40.00**	**13.33**
Share with	-	-	-	-	-	-	00.00
colleagues	-	-	**35.00**	**10.00**	-	-	**7.50**
No Change	44.00	72.73	40.00	74.00	56.00	56.00	53.68
	40.00	**60.00**	**30.00**	**50.00**	**70.00**	**20.00**	**45.00**
Total	100.00	100.00	100.00	100.00	100.00	100.00	100.00
	100.00	**100.00**	**100.00**	**100.00**	**100.00**	**100.00**	**100.00**

Getting irritated and angry (18.38), was reported in largest percentages in 1990, (doctors-30.00% and engineers-22.00%). While in 2002, stress and tension (18.33) was reported, as a result of unpleasantness at home in largest perentage, doctors (40.00) and engineers (35.00) say in large percentage. Thus, doctors and engineers are seen to be more prone to change in mood because of any unpleasant incident at home.

Impact on professionals owing to their female status

This seeks to find out whether the professional being a female, is able to do the assigned work with preciseness and efficiency, or whether her being a female become a handicap. Whether she feels that her male colleagues are at an advantage with regards to the demands of the job and opportunities for growth.

Table : 5.10 : Impact of female status by their profession

Opinion about Female status helpful at the place of work	Profession						
	Medicine	**Law**	**Engineer-ing**	**Teaching**	**Nursing**	**Social work**	**Total**
No help	36.00 **10.00**	72.73 **90.00**	88.00 **100.00**	32.00 **40.00**	14.00 **40.00**	44.00 **60.00**	45.22 **56.66**
Yes,							
Women tend to be more affectionate	- -	- -	- -	14.00 **40.00**	8.00 **10.00**	- **10.00**	7.38 **19.23**
Female clients feel secured or gives preference	30.00 **25.00**	12.00 -	 -	6.00 -	2.00 **40.00**	- **20.00**	22.15 **23.38**
Female patients/clients more open	46.00 **65.00**	- -	- -	42.00 -	12.00 **10.00**	- -	20.13 **44.23**
Understands children better	- -	- -	- -	- **20.00**	- -	- **10.00**	- **11.43**
Greater acceptance by target group which is female	16.00 - -	33.00 **10.00**	- -	6.00 -	2.00 -	- 20.00	22.15 **8.84**
Canhandle delicate work	- -	- -	12.00 -	- -	- -	- -	4.38 -
Base	100.00 **100.00**	100.0 **100.0**	100.00 **100.00**	100.00 **100.00**	100.00 **100.00**	100.00 **100.00**	100.00 **100.00**

Majority of respondents in 2002 are of the view that their being a female is of no help to them (56.66) all the engineers (100.00) and large percentage of layers (90.00) hold this view.

While in 1990 only 45.22% respondnts said that their being a female didnot help in their professionals pursuit. There again engineers (88.00) and lawyers (72.73) are in higest percentages. Thus engineering and Law comes out as those professions which doesnot go with female status of the professional.

Amongst those who feel their being a famale professional is helpful in their profession, respondents, mainly from medical and nursing profession, said that their patients are more open and communicate their problems without any inhibition (20.13 and 44.23) because of being treated by female doctors (46.00 and 65.00) or nurses (12.00 and 10.00).

The profession of medicine and social work require the professional to be more patient and affectionate. A teacher who has to tackle a large number of students, to be successful, has to be patient, caring and affectionate, especially when dealing with small children. Social workers dealing with disabled children or clients, working in remand homes and other correctional institution have to show these attributes to be effective.

In the 1990 study, it is interesting to observe that professionals from the category of law also said that their clients give preference to lady lawyers, so as to assess their capability. But in 2002, many of the law professionals have this view that being a female lawyer is not of any help. Infact, a few of them even said that it has an adverse effect on their profession, and they have to put more effort in front of male judges to present and effectively prove their cases.

Another advantage of being a female professional is the acceptance by female beneficiaries is more (22.15 and 3.84). Doctors (46.00) and lawyers (33.00) said this is large percentages in 1990 study.

Respondents in good percentages are of the opinion that female clients feel secured or gives preference to women professionals (22.15 and 23.38). This opinion is shared by doctors (30.00 and 25.00), Lawyers (12.00 and 00.00), nurses (2.00 and 40.00) and social workers (00.00 and 20.00).

It has been observed in both the studies that most of the doctors were gyneacologists by specialization, who exclusively deal with female patients. As this branch needs close physical examination, the patients prefer going to a female doctor.

Social workers dealing with female clients in the field find that their gender is helpful in their profession.

CHAPTER 6

CAUSES OF ROLE CONFLICT

Every problem, what so ever it may be, is always associated with a cause. Various writers have expressed different views about the causation of social problems. Bhatia (1976: 07) writes about the cause of conflict among working women: *They are confronted with a situation where they have already opted for a job and entered a new role of a modern earning 'woman' changing the traditional role of a home maker which is her prime responsibility. This is the genesis of the problem when the traditional is not wholly abandoned and the modern is not being fully adopted*[1].

In the opinion of Kapoor (1975 : 30): *In this transitional era there is a role confusion because of the absence of harmony between her old and new roles, that of a worker and a housewife and mother, and also because of the tension that is created due to her inner conflict*[2].

According *to* Rastogi (1976 : 224): *The increasing sense of self importance, self assertion and individualism among the working women is responsible for inter-generational conflict in families of the working women*[3].

Lexicon Universal Encyclopedia (Vol. 16: 271) gives the following account. *When women achieve advancement in social structure outside the home, role conflict is created*[4]. And, according to the theory of causation of social problems, there is a multiplicity of factors, which can be held responsible for creating the problem of role conflict. Sood (1991: 95) is of the view that *employed women face the problem of adjustment because of their role expectations. They are required to perform multiple roles and at time conflicting roles*[5].

Survey of the available relevant literature shows that a number of factors, such as, different kinds of expectations of the family members in various aspects of their lives which they desire to be taken care of, and performance of multiple duties and responsibilities relating to fulfillment of various types of functions in the family, non-cooperation or lesser extent of help in her household jobs, dis-interest in the promotion of her career, the female status etc. adversely affect her career growth.

Small age group of children, work at office or home interfering in the other areas, night duty and its associated problems, specific types of persons creating special problems and no job satisfaction can be great causes of role conflict.

The role-conflict of working women, result to a great extent from the cleavage between the new social and economic goal (education and employment) and the rigid social structure. (Jha and Pujari (Ed.) 1996 : 150)[6].

Causes of role conflict can be broadly categorized under the following heads :

(a) **Family Causes :** Factors which lead to role conflict among working women and have the origin in the family set-up comes under this category, e.g., if the family has an unfavourable attitude towards her professional practice, or does not help her in her household chores and have no interest in the promotion of her career, will lead to roles conflict, and eventually adversely affect her performance and efficiency, at work place and at home as well.

Jha and Pujari ((Ed.) 1996 : 212) has reflected that *although the greatest problem of employed women emerge from the divergent demands which family and profession make on them and they occur mainly in the sphere of the family*[7].

(b) **Organizational Causes :** This includes those variables which come under the perview of causes related to workplace, and they create conflict in the different roles, which the working professional has to play, such as difficulties related to night duty, undue liberties taken by male employees at work place, and other such factors having their origin at the place of work.

(c) **Community Causes** : Here community plays a role in causing role conflict in working women. Community or society at large creates such situations which ultimately lead to role conflict, e.g., discriminatory social attitude of society towards working women, gossip and rumour mongering, wilful, slander campaigns etc.

Attitude of people at home towards the professional practice.

The kind of attitude the family of the woman has towards her professional pursuit can be a dired cause of conflict for her. The following figure throus light on the attitude of people at home towards the professional practice.

Fig : 6.1 : Comparision of attitude of people at home towards the professional practice.

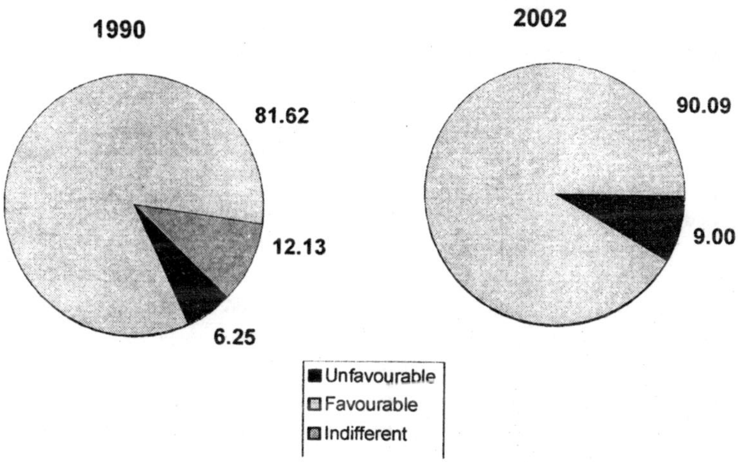

The figure project a very favourable situation for the working professional, in that, they find favourable attitude of people, in both the studies. The time span spent between the 1990 and 2002 studies have no bearing on the attitude of people in this regard.

Here it is relevant to recall Promilla Kapur's study, which shows that *the attitude of the husband, in so far as the wifes employment is concerned, is one of wanting or at least, of not minding their being employed*[8]. (Kapur 1970 : 406).

Relationship between family and professional responsibilities

For a working woman, home and place of work are the two main fronts where she has to shoulder responsibilities of important nature. There is a set pattern of expectations, both at home, as well as at the place of work.

People at home, at times, without recognizing the two different spheres of work, demand the same attention and time from her, as is demanded of a wife or a mother in a situation when she is not working.

At the work place also, there is no let up in work expectations; in case of private practice, there is financial loss and good will to watch out for. In such instances, the working woman is caught between the devil and the deep sea, not to talk of the storms upon the road, in the home and in the office. A working woman is beset by a sea of chaos, confusion and conflicts–it is a wonder that an average working woman professional is alive, kindling, sane and successful too !

Table : 6.2 : Nature of relationship between house hold responsibilties and professional duties by their profession.

Type of Profession	NATURE OF RELATIONSHIP				
	In conflict	Complementing each other	Neither complementing nor conflicting	Can't say	Total
Medicine	18.00 **20.00**	40.00 **30.00**	40.00 **50.00**	2.00 -	100.00 **100.00**
Law	9.09 **10.00**	54.55 **75.00**	36.36 **15.00**	- -	100.00 **100.00**
Engineering	18.00 -	38.00 **85.00**	44.00 **15.00**	- -	100.00 **100.00**
Teaching	6.00 **10.00**	32.00 **25.00**	50.00 **60.00**	12.00 **5.00**	100.00 **100.00**
Nursing	6.00 **10.00**	50.00 **50.00**	40.00 **40.00**	4.00 -	100.00 **100.00**
Social Work	0.00 -	42.00 **60.00**	44.00 **40.00**	4.00 -	100.00 **100.00**
Total	11.03 **8.23**	41.55 **54.16**	43.01 **36.66**	4.41 **0.93**	100.00 **100.00**

The table show a favourable climate of opinion for her working status, when the nature of relationship between the household responsibilities and professional responsibilities was studied. It is found that in the contemporary times the relationship has taken a positive turn in being complementing in nature (54.16), while it was neither conflicting nor complementing (43.01) in the 90's.

Table: 6.3 : Relationship between professional and household responsibilities by various attributes

Attitude of people at Home:					
	Relationship between professional & household responsibilities				
	In Conflict	complementing each other	Neither Conflicting Nor Complementing	Can't say	Total
Favourable	9.91	42.34	44.59	3.15	100.00
	7.33	**55.04**	**36.69**	**0.91**	**100.00**
Unvarourable	41.8	17.65	35.29	5.88	100.00
	18.18	**45.45**	**36.36**	-	**100.00**
Indifferent	3.03	48.48	48.48	-	100.00
	-	-	-	-	-

X^2 Cal = 18.75; Tab = 9.49; $p < 0.05$; df = 4

X^2 1.680 df = 3; $p > 0.05$

Type of Family:

Joint Family	7.69	36.92	50.00	5.39	100.00
	9.09	**36.36**	**52.72**	**1.81**	**100.00**
Nuclear Family	14.08	45.78	36.62	3.52	100.00
	7.69	**69.23**	**23.07**	-	**100.00**

X^2 (Cal) = 7.15 (Tab) = 7.81 $p > 0.05$ df = 3

X^2 14.34 df = 3 $P < 0.05$

Marital Status:

Unmarried	7.25	44.93	37.68	10.14	100.00
	-	**28.57**	**71.42**	-	**100.00**
Married	14.08	37.64	45.51	2.81	100.0
	13.63	**63.63**	**21.21**	**1.50**	**100.00**
Separated	-	66.67	33.33	-	100.00
	-	-	-	-	
Divorced	-	33.33	66.67	-	100.00
	-	**100.00**	-	-	**100.00**
Widow	-	68.75	31.25	-	100.00
	-	**100.00**	-	-	**100.00**

Number of Children:

No Child	17.95	20.51	61.54	-	100.00
	9.09	**72.72**	**18.18**	-	**100.00**
One Child	10.87	32.61	47.83	8.69	100.00
	31.51	**42.10**	**21.25**	**5.26**	**100.00**
2-3 Children	11.34	48.45	40.21	-	100.00
	7.14	**85.71**	**7.14**	-	**100.00**
More than 3 children	4.76	71.43	23.81	-	100.00
	-	**100.00**	-	-	**100.00**

X^2 Cal = 12.76; Tab = 12.59; $p < 0.05$; df = 9

X^2 **14.95 df = 9 $P > 0.05$**

Monthly income:

below Rs. 2000	11.50	35.5	39.40	6.10	100.00
	10.00	**50.00**	**40.00**	-	**100.00**
Rs. 2-5000	12.16	40.54	45.95	1.35	100.00
	3.22	**51.61**	**41.93**	**3.22**	**100.00**
Rs. 5-10,000	-	60.00	40.00	–	100.00
	5.88	**47.05**	**47.85**	–	**100.00**
Rs. 10,000 & above	–	-	-	–	–
	13.33	**62.22**	**24.44**	–	**100.00**

Decision Making

Self	10.10	51.52	36.36	2.02	100.00
	9.09	**72.72**	**15.15**	**3.03**	**100.00**
Husband	5.0	45.00	40.00	10.00	100.00
	33.33	**66.66**	-	-	**100.00**
Father	5.56	33.33	55.55	5.55	100.00
	-	-	**100.00**	-	**100.00**
Mother	16.67	16.67	-	-	100.00
	-	**11.26**	**87.11**	-	**100.00**
In-laws	42.86	22.22	68.70	-	100.00
	-	-	-	-	**100.00**
Joint decisions	14.61	38.20	42.70	4.49	100.00
	9.09	**63.63**	**27.27**	-	**100.00**

On studying the relationship between nature of relationship between household duties, responsibilities on one hand, and attitude of family members towards her working status on the other hand, the picture which emerges is :

The respondents in largest percent say that they receive favourable attitude and the nature of relationship is complementing (55.04) in the latter study, whereas in 1990, respondents in largest percent said that their family members have a favourable attitude and the nature of relationship is neither conflicting nor complementing (44.59).

Jha and Pujari ((Ed.) 1996 : 168) have also come out with the finding that *the majority of women live in a family atmosphere, which is positively disposed towards their professional pursuit*[9].

In 2002, only 18.18% respondents, whose relationship is conflicting face unfavourable attitude of their family members while 41.8% of the respondents faced unfavourable attitude in 1990. Thus, respondents receiving unfavourable attitude and find the two types of responsibilities in conflict have reduced to quite an extent.

Kiran Devendra's study is in contradiction here as when she writes : *With the spread of education women were trying to be both housewives and career women. This is not easy*[10]. *(1985 : 111)*

The result may not concur with this observation as in both the studies only a small percentage of professionals (11.03 and 8.23) of the total sample, have reported facing a conflicting situation.

Application of Chi-square test on 1990 data show that the two variables have an association while the same test when applied on 2002 data shows that the variables of attitude of people at home towards her professional practice and the nature of relationship between professional and domestic responsibilities have no association.

Type of Family

The type of family from which the working woman comes also plays a significant part in deciding what may be the kind of equation between the home and professional front. In a nuclear family, her routined interaction remains restricted to the spouse and the children, and she has responsibilities towards a fewer members, than in a joint family. While in a joint famliy there is multiplicity of roles, where every member's expectation of role fulfilment may be different.

The social institution of the joint family, on the whole, discouraged the independence and initiative of its members. This is especially marked in case of women[11]. ("Devendra Kiran, 1985 : 2). Professionals coming from joint family say in largest percentage that their nature of relationship is neither conflicting nor complementing (50.00 and 52.72), while professionals from nuclear family, in largest percentages, report the relationship to be complementing each other (45.78 and 69.23).

This suggest that professionals from nuclear family, contribute in majority to the family resources, thereby making significant addition, whereas, in a joint family system, the resources may not have altered to an appreciable extent because of the working women's contribution.

The conflicting relationship was faced by professionals from nuclear family in maximum percentages in the earlier study (14.08), and in the recent times, the picture has changed and professionals from joint family face conflicting situation in larger percentages (9.09).

Kapoor's (1970 : 67) observation concurs with the earlier study. She comes to a conclusion that *the joint family today has a positive effect on marital adjustment of working women*[12].

The analysis of the data shows that, in 1990, nuclear family posed more conflicting situation for a professional working woman, while in 2002, expectations in a joint family are difficult to be met.

Chi square test when applied on the two sets of data has shown different results. In 1990, the test shows that there is no dependence between the attributes i.e. type of family from which the professionals hail, and the nature of relationship bear no significance, while the test when applied on 2002 data, shows that the two variables are significant to each other.

Marital Status

Nature of relationship is than seen with respect to the marital status of the professionals. That is, in which of the marital statuses, viz., married, separated, divorced etc., do women face conflict in maximum percentages and in which of the marital statuses do women find the variables complementing each other.

In the 2002 study, all the divorced professionals (100.00) say that the nature of relationship is complementing while in 1990 study, a large percent of widows and separated professionals (60.75 and 66.67), reported to have complementing relationship.

Widow professionals in both the studies have opined that they have a complementing relationship between the two types of responsibilities. More married professionals are now of the opinion that their responsibilities at the two fronts complement each other, which is a change from the earlier opinion of married women. The opposite trend is observed with regards to the unmarried professionals, who said that they have neither complementing nor conflicting relationships, in the 2002 study, while in 1990 largest percentage said that their relationship is complementing.

On comparing the two studies one can see that in 2002 more percentage of married professionals (63.63) find the two type of responsibilities complementing where as 12 years ago, it was the unmarried professionals, (44.93) who professed to have complementing relationship.

The percentage of professionals saying that the two types of responsibilities are in conflict (14.08 and 13.63) belong to the married category, percentage being almost same in both the studies.

In the 2002 no other category of professionals face conflicting situation, whereas in 1990, a small percent of respondents (7.25) came from unmarried category as well.

Number of Children

This is to study the impact of the variable, number of children the professional has, and the nature of relationship which exists between the home and professional front.

With children, the demands on the mother becomes more and responsibilities at home multiply. Apart from addition to the family income, the other attributes which she learns or imbibes, by virtue of being a professional are - a teacher understands the psychology of the children better, a doctor becomes a good role model of being helpful and compassionate, nurses and social workers understanding the psychology of people and being more affectionate and patient with the clients may said to be supplementing the relationship with children at home.

The empirical studies show the following picture.

When the number of children is more, complementing relationship emerge in the largest percentage, in both the studies (71.43 and 100.00). But in 2002 when the professionals has no child, then also complementing relationship has been professed in large percentage (72.72).

Conflicting relationship emerged in small percentages, in each of the four categories of professionals, with respect to number of children in 1990 study, while in 2002, although there is no incidence of conflicting relationship when the professional, have more than three children. But in the other three categories, the percentage is seen to be largest in the category of one child (31.51).

Thus the results of both the studies reflect the same picture; that number of children does not seem to have any relationship with the nature of the two types of responsibilities.

On applying chi square test on 1990 data, it show that the two attributes are associated with each other while on 2002 data, the test show that the results have no association.

Monthly income and the nature of relationship

Within a span of 12 years, the monthly income of the professionals increased manifold; in the earlier study no professional was ready to accept that her monthly income was more than Rs. 10,000/-, although some of the doctors were leading practitioners and run their own big nursing homes. In the later study, a good percent of professionals conceded that their monthly income is more than Rs. 10,000/-, per month.

The two variables were assessed in relation to one another, to see that, when the monthly income is high or substantial, does it make the relationship complementing, and vice-versa.

In 2002 study 62.22 of professionals earning Rs. 10,000/-, and above said that their relationship is complementing, while in 1990 study a large percent of professionals (60.00) said that their relationship is complementing when they were earning between Rs. 5-10,000/-, per month.

Professionals claim neither conflicting nor complementing relationships in very consistent percentage (between 39 to 48) in the two studies irrespective of the time span between the two.

Professionals confirming of conflicting relationships is found to be scattered in all the four income groups in 2002 study, while in 1990 study, the higher income group had no incident of conflicting relationship. Thus one can say that in 90's, high monthly income of the professional reduced the conflicting nature of relationship between her professional and home fronts whereas in 21st century the monthly income of the professional has no effect on the type of relationship that exists between the two diametrically opposite spheres of her life.

Decision maker in the family

The two variables are tabulated with reference to each other to find out who is the decision taking authority, when the relationship between domestic and professional relationship is in conflict or when it is complementing.

The role of the professional remains important when it comes to taking decisions in the family matters, and the complementing relationship (51.52 and 72.72) clearly emerges out of the two studies, when only the professional herself is instrumental in taking decision.

When joint decisions are taken, again the trend remains the same. A good percent of professionals professed to have complementing relationship (38.20 and 63.63).

Conflicting relationship is projected in the largest percentage, in 2002, when the decisions are being taken by the husband (33.33) and in 1990, it was the in-laws (42.86) who were taking decisions in the family.

It is interesting to note that conflicting relationship has also been reported, even though in small percent, when she herself is the decision maker, or does it jointly. Both the studies show the same trend – self (10.10 and 9.09), and joint decisions (14.61 and 9.09).

Reaction of the family members if professional practice was not taken up

Attitude of family members towards the professional practice of a woman is an important derivative in creating or lessening of role conflict for the women. On the other hand, reaction of the family members, if she would not have taken up her professional practice, inspite of her educational background, can serve as a good indicator of creating or lessening of role conflict. If the family welcomes her sitting at home, that means the family's not cooperating, or cooperating under compulsion. And, if the family condemns her action of sitting at home, it will help her in sorting out problem arising out of taking up of the profession.

Table : 6.5 : Reaction of the family in relation to other variables

Profession

	Reaction of the family			
	Would have Welcomed it	**Would have condemned**	**Neither welcomed Nor condemmed it**	**Total**
Medicine	12.00 **20.00**	44.00 **60.00**	44.00 **20.00**	100.00 **100.00**
Law	13.57 **-**	22.68 **45.00**	63.64 **55.00**	100.00 **100.00**
Engineering	8.00 **15.00**	40.00 **85.00**	52.00 **-**	100.00 **100.00**
Teaching	20.00 **10.00**	22.00 **30.00**	58.00 **60.00**	100.00 **100.00**
Nursing	22.00 **10.00**	42.00 **40.00**	38.00 **50.00**	100.00 **100.00**
S. work	12.00 **-**	10.00 **50.00**	78.00 **50.00**	100.00 **100.00**
Total	13.97 **9.16**	30.15 **51.66**	54.78 **39.16**	100.00 **100.00**

Attitude of people at home

Favourable	63.16 **100.00**	82.93 **95.08**	85.53 **100.00**
Unfavourable	26.32 **-**	4.88 **4.91**	1.97 **-**
Indifferent	10.52 **-**	12.19 **-**	12.50 **-**
Total	100.00 **100.00**	100.00 **100.00**	100.00 **100.00**

X^2 (Cal)= 30.73, Tab=9.49 $p<0.05$, df=4

X^2= 2.976, df=2 $p>0.05$

Nature of Relationship

In conflict	23.68 **-**	10.98 **9.67**	8.05 **8.5**
Complementary	34.21 **18.18**	57.32 **67.74**	33.56 **44.68**
Neither conflicting nor complementary	42.11 **36.36**	20.05 **20.96**	52.35 **57.44**
Can't say	- **9.09**	3.65 **-**	6.04 **-**
Total	100.00 **100.00**	100.00 **100.00**	100.00 **100.00**

X^2 (Cal)= 21.12, Tab=9.49 $p<0.05$, df=6

X^2= 22.32, df=6 $p>0.05$

The comparison of the empirical data shows that the family of the professional has become particular about her pursuing her profession, in the past 12 years. In 1990, largest percentage of professionals had this view that if they would not have chosen to work in their profession, their family would have neither welcomed, not condemned, their decision (54.78). While in 2002, the largest percentage (51.66) of professionals have opined that their family would not have appreciated their decision to opt out of their profession.

For condemning reaction percentage was good 30.15% in 1990, but it has increased by more than 20.00% over a period of a decade. Engineers (85.00), doctors (60.00), and social workers (50.00), report condemning of opinion in high percentage in 2002, while doctors (44.00), nurses (42.00), and engineers (40.00) reported condemning by their family in the 1990 study.

In 1990 a small percentage of professionals (13.97) reported of their sitting at home been welcomed by their family, the percentage further decline to 9.16% in 2002. Nursing professional (22.00), said this in highest percentage in 1990, while medical practitioners said this in highest percentage (20.00) in 2002.

It is a general observation from the collected data that more rigorous is the training and difficult is the admission into the professional course, higher is the percentage of professional reporting condemning attitude of the family.

It points to one conclusion that the families also want the women to pursue their profession when they worked hard to get trained and spent so much of money, effort and time on it.

Attitude of people at home towards the professional practice and reaction of the family if the professional was not pursuing her profession

When the two variables are studied in relation to each other it is found in both the studies that a large percent of professionals say that they see favourable attitude of their family and that their family would have condemned their decision of not taking up professional practice (82.93 and 95.08).

But in 2002 study, all those professional whose family would have hither to welcomed their not working status, show favourable attitude towards their professional practice. The percentage is high in 1990 also

(63.16). Same is the scene with professionals reporting neither welcomed nor condemned opinion. This type of contradiction is also supported by X^2 test, the result of which says that the two variables show no significance, when applied on 2002 data.

While in 1990, less percent of professionals (4.88) reported unfavourable attitude and condemning reaction. This is slightly lower than 2002 percentage (4.91). Women in more percentages reported of unfavourable attitude and welcomed reaction (26.32) indifferent altitude and welcomed reaction (10.52) in 1990.

But, on applying X^2 test on 1990 data, the result says that the two variables show a positive association. It shows no association on 2002 data.

Nature of relationship and reaction of the family

When nature of relationship between professional and domestic responsibilities is studied in relation to the reaction of the family if the respondents were not working, both the studies have highest percentage of professions saying complementing relationship and condemning reaction, if not working (57.32 and 67.74). This suggests that when the two type of responsibilities are complementary in nature, the professionals have family support to take up their careers.

The next category with good percentage is of professionals professing neither conflicting nor complementary relationship and neither welcomed nor condemned reaction if not working (52.35 and 57.44).

When the professionals feels that the relationship is conflicting, a good percentage of respondents in 1990 said that their family would have welcomed their not pursuing their professional (23.68).

Undue liberties taken by male employees

Many a times, in news papers and magazines we come across incidences of harassment of women employees by the male staff. Such incidences are more common in professions where interactions with male employees is more and for long hours; or in male dominated professions like law where the males out number the females. The woman has to work along with her male colleagues and subordinates. It is a natural human tendency to develop certain affinity within a small group, with whom she spends her not so busy time. This group may comprise of her superiors, subordinates, colleagues juniors. Till it's a healthy relationship, it goes well. But when the males in the group want to take undue advantage of her female status, conflict arises.

At times, because of jealousy among the males, towards the female professionals, they start taking undue liberties which when in excess may lead to frustration for the woman. Thus a conflict or stressful situation may arise out of it.

On probing the incidences of undue liberties taken by the male employees at the place of work, the following picture emerges :

Table : 6.5 : Incidences of undue liberty by the profession

Both the studies reveal that professionals do not face the threat of

Incidences of undue liberty	Medicine	Law	Engnerring	Teaching	Nursing	Social work	Total
Yes	6.00	18.18	52.00	4.00	22.00	12.00	19.12
	10.00	**20.00**	**15.00**	-	**10.00**	-	**10.83**
No	82.00	81.82	48.00	76.00	78.00	88.00	75.00
	70.00	**80.00**	**85.00**	**100.00**	**90.00**	**100.00**	**85.33**
Not Applicable	12.00	-	-	20.00	-	-	5.88
	20.00	-	-	-	-	-	**3.33**
Total	100.00	100.00	100.00	100.00	100.00	100.00	100.00

Persons taking undue liberty.

	Higher ups	colleagues	subordinates	visitors	any other
1990	42.31	48.08	17.31	3.85	5.77
2002	**61.53**	**15.38**	**23.07**	-	-

undue liberties being taken, at large. Only in small percent, the professionals say that they have to face such a problem. From teaching and social work, none of the professionals face this problem in 2002 study, while in 1990, respondents from social work (88.00), and medicine (82.00) in largest percentages, professed of not facing the problem of unwarranted behaviour from men folk around them.

In 1990, 52.00% of engineering professionals reported having to face undue liberties being taken with, and in 2002, it's the law professionals

(20.00), who face this conduct from their colleagues and seniors in largest percentages.

When it was probed as to who these people were, who try to take undue liberty of the female professionals, the highest percent in 1990 constituted of colleagues (in 48.08), and in recent one, it was the higher ups (61.53), who pose this problem in largest percentages at the place of work. Jha and Pujari (Ed :1996 : 212) writes that *many colleagues do not know that how they should behave in wake of women employees working with them*[13].

Any one could have been the offender, said 5.77% of those who faced this problem in 1990. On comparing the two studies it can be seen that in the earlier one colleagues were the most potent agents to take undue liberties, while seniors or higher ups emerged as the offenders in the recent one .

In 2002 study, the undue liberties are in the nature of persistently asking for eating out or watching a film and long unwarrented conversations. Most of the professionals who faced the problem in 2002 study, come from the profession of law (46.15) and then from engineering (23.07) Medicine and Nursing (15.38 from each profession). Teaching and social work professionals reported no such incidence.

Nursing and medical professionals faced the problem of harassment which is compounded by their odd hour duty schedules. One of the law professional said that the males in the profession look forward to full entertainment and the females have to tactfully avoid such a situation.

The professionals when faced by this type of a situation, say that they avoid the offence by pretending not to understand, or by side tracking the issue, as the reaction to such undue liberties.

In 1990 study, the female professionals were most of the time subjected to listening of unwarranted comments (65.38 of engineering professionals), and unnecessary 'lifts' like talking unnecessarily and persistently (law professionals 100.00). Other problems were leg pulling, trying to find out family loopholes, back biting with bosses, talk vulgar and pass cheap comments and making financial manipulation and harassment. In both the studies it has been reported that frequency of such happenings is only sometimes (100.00 in 2002, and 63.46 in 1990).

Job Satisfaction

It forms an integral part of the professional's life. At times, because of various reasons, she does not get the desired satisfaction out of her professional pursuit. But, she cannot leave the job as it may lead to economic hardships, or it's not possible to find another job which is more suitable for her. With job satisfaction comes perfection, efficiency, and willingness to put more effort in the pursuit.

Respondents of these studies had to devote considerable time period in skill development while getting trained for a particular profession. In this context it becomes important and pertinent to assess the level of job satisfaction of the professionals.

Table : 6.6 : Level of job satisfaction of the respondent by their profession

Level of job Satisfaction	Medicine	law	Enginerring	Teaching	Nursing	Social work	Total
Satisfying	56.00	90.91	28.00	74.00	78.00	46.00	59.19
	80.00	**85.00**	-	**90.00**	**80.00**	**60.00**	**65.83**
Not wholly satisfying	40.00	4.09	66.00	24.00	22.00	48.00	37.50
	10.00	**15.00**	**100.00**	**10.00**	**20.00**	**40.00**	**32.00**
Dissatisfying	4.00	-	2.0	-	-	4.00	1.47
	10.00	-	-	-	-	-	**1.66**
Indifferent	-	-	4.00	2.00	-	2.00	1.47
	-	-	-	-	-	-	-
Total	100.00	100.00	100.00	100.00	100.00	100.00	100.00
	100.00	**100.00**	**100.00**	**100.00**	**100.00**	**100.00**	**100.00**

Both the studies have professionals saying in majority, that they are satisfied with their current job (59.19 and 65.83). This has also been the findings of London School of Economics Survey conducted in 1970. Professionals have stated it in large percentages, in 2002, except those from engineering, where all the professionals (100.00) stated of not wholly satisfying job profile.

As stated earlier, these professionals were drawn from government offices where the job is monotonous and there are very bleak promotional chances. Same is the case of social workers, working under governmental dictats, wherein both the studies, this opinion has been recorded (48.0 and 40).

Both the studies have engineering (66.00 and 100.00) and social work (48.00 and 40.00) professionals reporting of not wholly satisfying job profile in high percentages. Medicine is the only profession where professionals have reported dissatisfaction with their job in both the studies (4.00 and 10.00), and their percentage has increased in 2002.

Reference

1. Bhatia, Pratima : Role Conflict Among Working Women, Unpublished Ph.D. Thesis of Lucknow University (1976, p. 07).
2. Kapoor, Promilla : Marriage and the Working Women in India, Vikas Publishing House, New Delhi (1975, p. 30).
3. Rastogi, Shail Bala : Working Women in an Urban Setting, Unpublished Ph.D. Thesis of Lucknow University (1976, p. 224).
4. Lexicon Universal Encyclopaedia, New York, Lexicon publication, Vol. 16, p. 271.
5. Sood, Rita : Changing Status and Adjustment of Women, Manak Publication Pvt. Ltd. Jaipur/Delhi. (1991 p. 95).
6. Jha and Pujari (Ed.) : Indian women today Volume 3, Kanishka Publishers, New Delhi (1996, p.150).
7. abid (p. 212)
8. Kapoor, Promilla : Marriage and the Working Women in India, Vikas Publishing House, New Delhi (1970, p. 406).
9. Jha and Pujari (Ed.) : Indian women today Volume 3, Kanishka Publishers, New Delhi (1996, p. 168).
10. Devendra, Kiran: Status and Position of Women in India, Vikas Publishing House, Ghaziabad (1985, p. 111).
11. Ibid (p. 2)
12. Kapoor, Promilla : Marriage and the Working Women in India, Vikas Publishing House, New Delhi (1970, p. 67).
13. Jha and Pujari (Ed.) : Indian women today Volume 3, Kanishka Publishers, New Delhi (1996, p. 212).

CHAPTER 7

EFFECTS OF ROLE CONFLICT

Every conflicting situation leads to a number of adaptive and maladaptive consequences on the person who undergoes it. In case of female professionals also, it is but natural that the role conflict may extend to a number of effects, not only on their personality, but also on the all overall effectiveness of their functioning in different social settings right from the basic social institution of the family, to the organisation in which they work.

The Blackwell Dictionary of sociology (2000) reflects that there are a variety of responses for resolving or minimizing the effects of role conflict.

The first is to choose which role is most important and then isolate the expectations associated with the other role.

A second response is to leave one of the conflicting status (e.g. a woman quitting the job if it interferes too much with parenting responsibilities).

Third is role regeneration – the practice of separating various roles from one another (e.g. doctors do not treat their family members).

Fourth response is, what Erring Goffman called role distancing – a method of minimizing role strain associated with a disagreeable role.

It is against this background that information regarding multiplicity of effects of role conflict was gathered from the respondents and is being discussed in detail in the ensuing paragraphs.

Effect of remaining out on house-hold work

A woman who has to shoulder so many responsibilities at home and takes up professional responsibilities as well, has to divide her time for both the demanding parts of her life. If she neglects her house-hold duties and has no other person to take care at home, then her home is in a state of mess, and if she neglects her professional responsibilities, then her career is jeopardized.

Being cautious in her judgment and knowing how to strike a balance, both the fronts can be tackled without much problem.

Fig 7.1 : Effect of remaining out on house-hold work

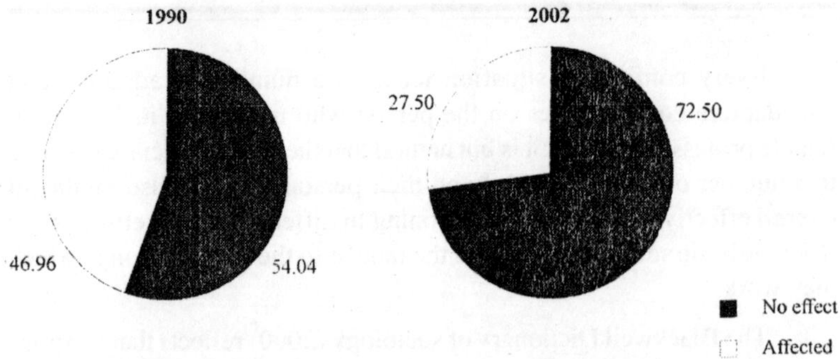

To find out what the professionals themselves feel about remaining out for professional pursuit affecting her house hold duties, the data from the two studies shows that a majority of professional (54.04 and 72.50) feel that their remaining out for work has no effect on their house hold responsibilities. Their profession wise break up runs as medicine (46.00 and 50.00) law (72.73 and 90.00), engineering (32.00 and 65), teaching (68.00 and 60), nursing (62.00 and 90.00), and social work (54.00 and 80.00). The statistics show that in 2002 study, there has been a phenomenal rise in percentages of professionals opting no effect, showing that the professionals work management has improved over a period of time.

In 1990, 46.96% and 27.50% respondents in 2002 are of the opinion that their remaining out does affect their house-hold responsibilities. Amongst them, care of children (46.40 and 75.75) was the major area of neglect: medicine (62.96 and 80) and social work (34.78 and 50) professionals opine this in large percentages in both the studies.

In 1990, other professionals reporting neglect of children, – law (33.33), engineering (47.56), teaching (17.65), nursing (47.37).

Another affected area reported is neglect of house hold work, general up keeping and management of house hold, leading to wastage (41.60 and 24.24). Again in 2002, only medicine (20.00) and social workers (50.00) have this opinion while in 1990, females from all the professions held the above opinion–law (66.67), engineering (29.41), teaching (17.65), nursing (15.79) and social work (60.8).

The comparative analysis suggest that the professionals of today get more help either from the family members, or servants, so as not to affect their domestic responsibilities.

Other areas of neglect cited in 1990 study were, cooking (35.5) maximum percentage from medicine (51.85), and teaching (50.00); cleanliness of the house (16.80); nursing (26.32), medicine (25.92); hobbies neglected (11.20), care of guests (7.20).

On applying chi-square test on 1990 data the values were X^2 (cal)= 19.34, tab=11.07, $p<.05$ df=5. When applied on 2002 data, the value came out to be 13.92 when $p < 0.05$ and df=5. In both the studies the two variables of effect on house hold responsibilities and profession bear a significant relationship.

When the variable of effect on dischange of house hold duties was studied with reference to the type of family and age group of children of the respondents the following picture emerges.

Table : 7.2 : Effect on house hold duties by type of family

Effect on house hold duties	Type of family		
	Joint	Nuclear	Total
Affected	38.46	57.04	48.16
	32.72	**18.46**	**25.00**
Not affected	61.54	42.96	51.84
	57.27	**81.53**	**75.00**
Total	100.00	100.00	100.00
	100.00	**100.00**	**100.00**

X^2 (Cal= 9.38; (tab)= 3.84, df= 1, $p<0.05$

X^2 = 3.234 , df= 1, $p>0.05$

It is generally believed that in a joint family system the work load may be more but the responsibilities and duties are shared among different members of the family. If there is an emergent situation or contingency with any member of the family, his/her duties are taken care of by other family members. While the quantum of work is less in a nuclear family, all the domestic duties have to be taken care of by the few members of the family.

It is with this view to find out if type of family and effect on house hold chores because of professionals remaining out for pursuing their careers their profession, has any relationship between them.

The empirical data show that professionals in very large percentages report that their house hold jobs are not affected. It is more evident in 2002 study (75.00), here 57.27% of them come from joint family while 81.53% of those living in nuclear family confrom to not affected opinion.

In 1990 study, more percentage of professionals from nuclear family (57.04), reported of their house hold jobs being affected while in 2002, it is the professional coming from joint family, say that their house-hold duties are neglected (32.72).

Application of chi-square test on 1990 data show that the two variables are dependent which is supported by empirical data while chi-square when applied on 2002 data show no dependence of the two variables which is again supported by the field data.

If women have to shoulder a score of responsibilities at home with different age-group of children, do these duties and responsibilities vary? Do the responsibilities at home have any relationship with the age-group of children?

Table : 7.3 : Effect on house hold duties by age group of children

Effect on house hold duties	Age group of children				
	upto 2 yrs.	3-5 yrs.	6-14 yrs.	More than 14 yrs	Total
Affected	73.68	56.92	48.65	50.00	53.60
	100.00	**57.14**	**30.00**	**56.25**	**49.38**
Non-affected	26.32	43.08	51.35	50.00	46.40
	-	**42.85**	**70.00**	**43.75**	**50.62**
Total	100.00	100.00	100.00	100.00	100.00
	100.00	**100.00**	**100.00**	**100.00**	**100.00**

X^2 (Cal= 4.43; (tab)= 7.81, df= 3, p>0.05

X^2 = 10.557, df= 3, p<0.05

Data from both the studies show the same trend that as the children become older, percentage of professionals reporting affected house hold responsibilities decrease and percentages of not affected category increase. Exception to this is the last age group when the children are more than 14 years of age. Maximum percentages of affected option appear when the age-group of children is less than 2 years (73.68 and 100.00) and maximum percentage of professionals reporting not-affected have children in the age group of 6-14 years (51.35 to 70.00).

Application of X^2 test on 1990 data show no significant relationship while the same test when applied on 2002 data shows a significant relationship between effect on house hold duties and responsibilities and the age-group of the children of the professionals.

If not doing professional practice, family affairs better managed or not

This question was administered to the respondents to find out the effect of pursuing her profession on family affairs – do they feel that had they not been doing their professional practice their home affairs would have been better managed.

Table : 7.4 : Management of house hold affairs, had they not been working by the type of profession :

Could have been better managed	Profession						Total
	Medicine	Law	Engineering	Teaching	Nursing	Social work	
Yes	46.00	27.27	50.00	30.00	28.00	42.00	38.23
	40.00	**5.00**	-	**15.00**	**10.00**	**20.00**	**15.00**
No	48.00	72.73	50.00	68.00	72.00	48.00	58.15
	50.00	**95.00**	**100.00**	**85.00**	**90.00**	**80.00**	**83.33**
Can't say	6.00	-	-	2.00	-	10.00	3.31
	10.00	-	-	-	-	-	**1.66**

X^2 (Cal)= 9.3; (tabulated)= 11.07, df= 10, p>0.05

X^2= 27.13, df= 10, p<0.05

The field data in both the studies show that professionals in majority say that their family affairs wouldn't have been better managed if they were not pursuing their profession. Majority, 58.45% professionals said this in 1990, while a larger percentage (83.33%) report the same in 2002.

Profession wise break up runs as medicine (48.00 and 50.00), law (72.73 and 90.00), engineering (50.00 and 100.00), teaching (68.00 and 85.00) nursing (72.00 and 95.00), and social work (48.00 and 80.00).

In 1990, 38.23% respondents and 15.00% respondent in 2002 report of their family affairs being better managed, if not in pursuance of their profession. Percentages are higher in 1990 data. Medicine – 46.00%, law– 27.27%, engineering – 50.00%, teaching – 30.00%, nursing – 28.00%, social work – 42.00%. In 2002 data, medicine – 40.00%, law – 5.00%, teaching – 15.00%, nursing – 10.00% and social work – 20.00% respondents were of this view.

In both the studies profession of medicine is the only one where professionals in good percentages say that if not in profession, their family affairs would have been better managed. It is the only profession where opinion in can't say category also appears although in small percentages 6.00% in 1990, and 10.00% in 2002 study.

So, it can be concluded that only in the profession of medicine the professionals feel that their house-hold affairs don't get sufficient time and attention because of their being in the profession.

Application of X^2 test shows a non-significant relationship on 1990 data while the relationship is found to be very significant on 2002 data (p=0.025).

When the attribute of family affairs being better managed if not working was studied in relation to other variables like attitude of family members towards the professional pursuit of the professional, number and age-group of the children the trends which emerge from the collected data show :

Table : 7.5: Different attributes by the opinion of the professionals (towards management of family affairs had they not taken up professional practice).

Attitude of family members

	Opinion of the respondent			Total
	Would have been better management	No effect	Can't say	
Favourable	37.84 **15.25**	59.01 **83.50**	3.15 -	100.00 **100.00**
Unfavourable	52.94 **100.00**	35.29 -	11.77 -	100.00 **100.00**
Indifferent	33.33 -	66.67 -	- -	100.00 -

X^2 (Cal) = 1.9, (tab)= 3.99, p>0.05, df = 4
X^2 (Cal) = 10.17, p<0.05, df = 2

Number of children

No Children	41.03 -	56.41 **77.77**	2.56 **22.22**	100.00 **100.00**
One Child	60.87 **50.00**	34.78 **50.00**	4.35 -	100.00 **100.00**
2-3 children	40.21 **31.11**	55.67 **68.88**	4.12 -	100.00 **100.00**
More than 3 children	23.81 -	66.67 **100.00**	9.52 -	100.00 **100.00**

X^2 (Cal) = 9.39, (tab)= 7.81, p<0.05, df = 6

X^2 (Cal) = 22.668, p<0.05, df = 6

Age group of children

Upto 2 yrs.	73.68 **60.00**	26.32 **40.00**	-	100.00 **100.00**
3-5 yrs.	47.69 **28.57**	52.31 **71.42**	- -	100.00 **100.00**
6-14 yrs	35.14 **16.66**	58.11 **83.33**	6.75 -	100.00 **100.00**
Above 14 yrs	31.25 **21.87**	59.38 **78.12**	9.37 -	100.00 **100.00**

X^2 (Cal) = 13.19, (tab)= 7.81, p<0.05, df = 6
X^2 (Cal) = 4.738, p>0.05, df = 3

Attitude of family members and management of house hold affairs if not working

In both the studies, professionals in large percentages report of favourable attitude of family members for their professional pursuit and no effect of her not doing her professional practice to manage family affairs in a better way. (59.01 in 1990 and 83.50 in 2002).

On the other hand, professionals opining family affairs would have been better managed if not working show high percentages in both the studies in the category of facing unfavourable attitude towards her going out for work (52.94 and 100.00).

On applying X^2 test, the relationship between the two variables show no significant relationship on 1990 data and the two variables are highly significant in 2002 study (p=0.00062) which is supported by the field data also.

Family affairs better managed if not working and number and age group of children

The responsibiliy of looking after the children rest primarily on the shoulders of the mother. Mother, if working, has to make adjustments and compromises so as to compensate for her working status. Children need time and attention. With major part of the day spent in professional pursuit, does it have any impact on bringing up of the children. Does her not taking up her profession, lead to better management of her family affairs, when studied in relation to the number and age group of children show the following result.

Both the studies show the same trend – more is the number of children, higher is the percentage of professionals reporting no effect. On the other hand, as the number of children increases, professionals reporting would have been better managed is reducing in both the studies. Thus, an inverse relationship between the two variables emerge on analysis of the filed data of the two studies.

On applying X^2 test on both the data, a positive dependency is seen in both the studies and in 2002 the relationship comes out to be highly dependent on each other but the gathered data have a different story to tell.

When the data were seen in relation to the age-group of children and family affairs better managed if not taken up the profession both the studies show the same pattern; as the age-group of children increases, would have been better managed percentages decreases. It is the same pattern when the professionals report of no effect. As the age group of children increases the percentage of respondents opining no effect also increases. Thus the two attributes show a significant relationship according to the field data.

Application of X^2 test on 1990 data show a significant relationship while on 2002 data X^2 test show no significant relationship which is not the case with empirical findings.

Reaction of the children

Children become the primary focus of attention for the parents and more so for the mother as the child is entirely dependent on her. For the first few months of infancy, she nurtures the child for all the possible needs. The child becomes an integral part of the life of the woman. For the child also, the world revolves round the mother. The child accepts her as the natural care-taker for all practical purposes whether the needs are physical, emotional or psychological. In this context, if the mother has to remain away from home for eight to ten hours of the day, it is sure to have an effect on the child.

Talwar's (1984) writes that a woman with a dual job is unable to give children either physical care, the direct supervision or the psychological response that they actually need and the result is emotional and behaviour problems of children.

But the present studies have different findings. A lot depends on the grooming of the child by the parents, how the child is prepared for this situation.

Table : 7.6 : Relation between reaction of the children and other variables

Profession	Reaction of the children because of her remaining out for professional pursuit					Total
	Miss her a lot	Become used to and get adjusted	Makes no difference	Getting hostile	Enjoys the situation	
Medicine	25.64	66.57	2.56	5.13	-	100.00
	50.00	**50.00**	-	-	-	**100.00**
Law	-	60.00	40.00	-	-	100.00
	25.00	**50.00**	**25.00**	-	-	**100.00**
Engineering	43.48	52.17	4.35	-	-	100.00
	15.00	**75.00**	-	-	**10.00**	**100.00**
Teaching	15.39	76.92	7.69	-	-	100.00
	25.00	**50.00**	**25.00**	-	-	**100.00**
Nursing	20.00	60.00	20.00	-	-	100.00
	50.00	**50.00**	-	-	-	**100.00**
Social Work	6.45	80.65	12.90	-	-	100.00
	-	**100.00**	-	-	-	**100.00**
Total	20.12	67.07	11.59	1.22	-	100.00
	24.24	**65.15**	**7.57**	-	**3.03**	**100.00**

Type of family

Joint Family	25.00	60.00	12.00	2.66	-	100.00
	32.14	**53.17**	**14.28**	-	-	**100.00**
Nuclear family	15.38	73.62	10.98	-	-	100.00
	20.51	**69.23**	**2.56**	-	**33.33**	**100.00**

Age Group of Children

Upto 2 yrs.	52.63 **80.00**	42.11 **20.00**	5.26 -	- -	- -	100.00 **100.00**
2-5 yrs.	27.69 **45.67**	64.62 **54.28**	4.61 -	3.08 -	- -	100.00 **100.00**
6-14 yrs.	12.16 **16.66**	79.73 **83.33**	8.11 -	- -	- -	100.0 **100.00**
above 14 yrs.	4.69 **15.62**	81.25 **62.38**	14.06 **15.62**	- -	- **6.23**	100.00 **100.00**

Period of service

Just joined	100.00 **100.00**	- -	- -	- -	- -	100.00 **100.00**
Between 1-3 yrs.	42.86 **28.57**	42.86 **71.42**	14.28 -	- -	- -	100.00 **100.00**
Between 4-5 yrs.	60.00 **25.00**	20.00 **75.00**	20.00 -	- -	- -	100.00 **100.00**
More than 5 years	16.44 **32.14**	71.23 **65.35**	10.96 **9.92**	1.37 -	- **3.57**	100.00 **100.00**

Let us also study, what the respondents have to say about their children's reaction towards their staying away from home because of their professional practice.

In both the studies professionals in large majority are of the opinion that their children have become used to their going out for work and have adjusted to the situation (67.07 and 65.15). Both the studies have social workers saying this in largest percentages (80.65 and 100.00).

The percentage of respondents reporting that their children miss her during their absence is much small (20.12 and 24.24). In 2002, only medicine (50.00), and nursing (50.00), profession have good percentages in this category. It may be because of the fact that both these professions demand lot of time from the professional and require the presence of the professional at odd hours of the day, when the children want their mother to be with them (e.g. night duties require a stay in the hospital for one and a half days at a stretch).

In 1990, engineering professionals (43.48) said that their children miss them. In 1990 data as reported earlier, most of the professionals were working with PSUs, which require 8 hours duty plus commutting time. Thus, the time devoted to professional pursuit was more, when compared to other professions. They had less number of holidays also. These factors may have led to this kind of opinion for the engineering professionals.

Law professionals (40.00 and 25.00) in both the studies, report of their children being not affected by her absence or presence at home. Teachers (25.00 in 2002) and nurses (20.00 in 1990) have also opined in sizeable percentages about their children being unaffected by their absence or presence. Doctors (5.13% in 1990) even reported their children developing hostile tendencies because of her absence as a result of her professional pursuit. Engineers (10.00) in 2002 study profess that their children enjoy their going out for work as they have more independence.

It can be concluded that in both the studies, data shows that the children are gracious and adjust to the situation, when their mother goes for work without any fuss or being judgmental.

Type of family and of the children

When the same variable is studied with regards to the type of the family the professionals come, in both the type of families, joint (60.00 and 53.7) and nuclear (73.62 and 69.23) professionals in majority say that their children have become used to their working status. When the category of children missing the mother is seen, in both the studies, it is the joint family (25.00 and 32.14) where the percentages are more than the nuclear family.

Age Group of children and reaction of the children

Children need the care and attention of the mother at all ages but smaller the age-group of children, more is the attention they need. As they grow up and start going to school, they need less time and attention from the mother. They start understanding their own routine and even the routine of their parents–that mummy will remain out and for what part of the day, and when does papa come back from work.

The results of analysis of empirical data show that in both the studies, as the age group of children increases, percentage of professionals reporting that their children were getting used to their remaining out, also increases. In 2002, more than 14 years category is the only exception, the percentage is less than the 6-14 yrs. option.

Whereas when the category of children missing the professional is seen, it is observed that as the age group children's of increases, percentage of professionals reporting missing her a lot decreases.

Women's absence or presence at home is of no consequence in case of law professionals in the largest percentages, (40.00 and 25.00), in both the studies.

Period of service and reaction of the children

This is to study, when the period of service of the mother increases, do the children get more accustomed to her going out for work. The empirical data show that in both the studies all the respondents (100.00 and 100.00), report of their children missing her when the period of service has just commenced. The data in both the studies takes a roller coaster route, lowering of percentages in missing category in (1-3) years period, again rising in the categories of (4-5) years of service, and dipping in more than five years of service category (trend in 1990 study). In 2002, percentage come down as the period of the service increase. But again rises when period of service is more than 5 yrs. Up and down trend is observed in the category of children being used to and adjusted to the situation.

Thus the analysis of data does not show any clear relationship between reaction of the children and period of service of the professionals.

CHAPTER 8

ATTITUDES AND BELIEFS OF THE RESPONDENTS

Every person has got a typical personality structure, characterized by attitudes, beliefs, and personal convictions etc., which not only affect his/ her perceptions, but also considerably influence his or her actions. Attitudes are relatively enduring organisations, reflecting the mental readiness of the person to act or behave in a particular manner, in a given situation. Beliefs refer to that part of the cognitive world which may or may not be necessarily true, but are considered to be so, because of their transmission through various sources of knowledge.

Thus, attitudes and beliefs of any person play a determining role in influencing the pattern of behaviour. Also, attitudes and beliefs of a person are very important in any study of the present nature, mainly because unhealthy attitudes and beliefs relating to various types of roles in different social settings, particularly regarding new roles in work organisation, may create additional problems and difficulties for the female professional.

It is against this background that data regarding attitudes and beliefs of female professionals relating to various dimensions of role conflict were gathered.

Measurable change has appeared in the educated working women. Hence, it has become imperative on the part of the sociologists and social scientists to study the changing attitudes of women, particularity educated working women.[1] (Reddy 1986: 15).

Relation between the period devoted to professional practice and conflicts faced in discharging their family responsibility by the professional

This is to study the opinion of the professionals, with regards to the relationship between the number of years the professionals have put in their professional practice and conflicts or difficulties faced by them in discharging their domestic responsibilities i.e to say, the difficulties faced by the professionals in taking care of their family becomes more acute with the passage of time or, whether the difficulties are more when the professional first begin to pursue her profession.

This will also show that as the number of years put in by the woman, in the profession increases, do the people at home make adjustments accordingly, does the work at home become easier, and the woman herself becomes more adapt at handling the two fronts, or is it easy to handle responsibilities at the beginning of her career, than later. The result of collected field data show :

Fig : 8.1 : Relation between time period devoted and conflicts faced

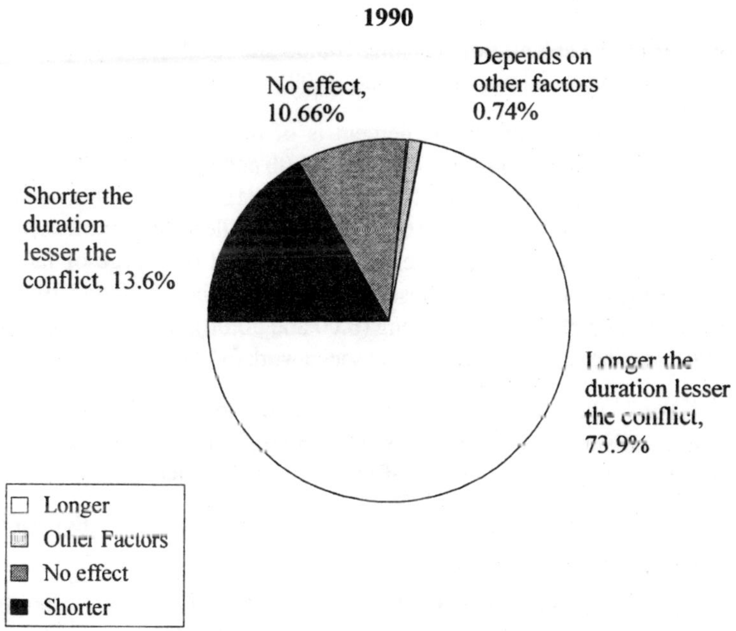

2002

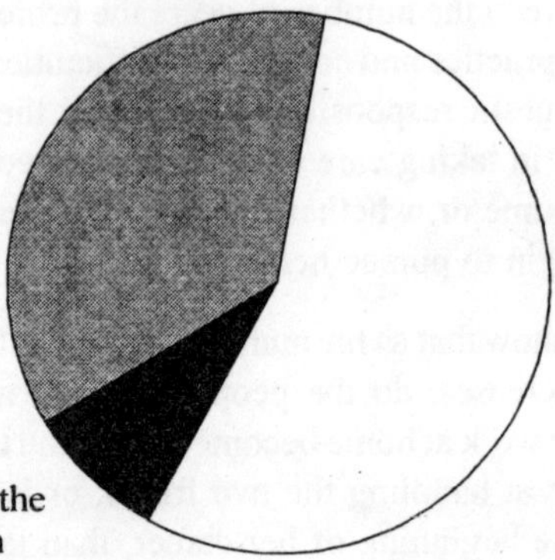

Both the studies have professionals opining in majority that longer the professional practice, lesser the conflict (73.90 and 55.83). Profession wise break-up runs as, medicine (64.00 and 60.00), law (81.82 and 75.00), engineering (82 and 40.00), teaching (68.00 and 40.00), Nursing (96.00 and 70.00), and social work (56.00 and 50.00).

In 1990, second largest percent is of those opining shorter the duration, less are the conflicts - doctors (24.00 and 20.00) law (00.00 and 00.00), engineering (10.00 and 10.00), teaching (12.00 and 10.00), nursing (2.00 and 00.00), social work (10.00 and 20.00). While in 2002, professionals professing no effect of time period devoted, and discharge of family responsibility is in second largest majority - medicine (8.00 and 20.00), law (18.18 and 20.00), engineering (6.00 and 50.00), teaching (4.00 and 50.00), nursing (2.00 and 30.00), and social work (34.00 and 43.00).

Thus, we can conclude that with the passage of time, the professionals in more percentages say that conflicts regarding domestic fronts have no relation to years of professional practice.

Professional Practice – at a stretch during the day or break - up in timings

It is to see if it is easier for the professional to take care of her family responsibilities when she works at a stretch, for the required number of hours during the day, or when the working hours are broken-up in two different time periods of the day, as in case of doctors, who run their own clinics and work partly in the morning hours, and again in the evening hours.

Table : 8.2 : Extent of conflict in single or break-up timings by their profession

Extent of Role conflict	Profession						
	Medicine	**Law**	**Engineering**	**Teaching**	**Nursing**	**Social work**	**Total**
More conflict in one time one	2.00 **10.00**	9.09 **35.00**	14.00 **10.00**	6.00 **25.00**	6.00	1.00 **30.00**	6.25 **18.33**
More conflict in many time duty	70.00 **20.00**	90.91 **60.00**	76.00 **90.00**	80.00 **70.00**	84.00 **90.00**	72.00 **50.00**	77.55 **63.33**
Equal conflicts in both	24.00 **50.00**	**5.00**	8.00	14.00	10.00 **10.00**	22.00 **20.00**	14.34 **14.16**
Can't say	4.00 **20.00**		2.00	**5.00**		4.00	1.84 **4.16**
Total	100.00 **100.00**	100.00 **100.00**	100.00 **100.00**	100.00 **100.00**	100.00 **100.00**	100.00 **100.00**	100.00 **100.00**

Data analysis of both the studies show that the majority of professionals have the opinion that there are more problems to sort out on home front, in more than one time duty (77.55 and 63.33). The reasons given were the adjustment to leave home has to be made twice in a day and there is wastage of time and money in commuting. More than that, people at home, especially children, know that once the mother is at home, she will remain with them for the rest of the day.

In 2002 (18.33) more percentage of professions than in 1990 (6.25) were of the opinion that there is more conflict in one time duty. Reason cited was–house-hold chores can be better managed. The husband may be there to take care of the children in the evenings. Whereas professionals opining equal conflicts in both type of duties is almost same in both the studies (14.34 and 14.16). The reasons given were in combination of the two categories ie, of one time and many time duty.

Employment versus private practice

The professional may be employed in an organisation where she has to work according to the set norms and parameters. It can be in the case of doctors and nurses, employed in any hospital/nursing home or lawyers taking up legal matters for the organisation. Professionally qualified social workers are employed in correctional and observation homes and in factories as welfare officers. But a professional can take up private practice as well like – doctors having their own clinic, teachers opening schools, lawyers taking up practice in courts. Social workers also work privately as counsellors and run their NGOs.

In both the situations the type of demands, from the professional is different. The effort here is to gather the opinion of the respondents as to where, whether in employment or private practice, do conflicts, faced by the professional in discharging her domestic responsibilities increase.

Table : 8.3 : Relative incidents of greater role conflict by professsion

Relative incidents	Profession						
	Medicine	Law	Engineering	Teaching	Nursing	Social work	Total
Employed professional face greater role conflict	28.00 **25.00**	9.09 **45.00**	18.00 **15.00**	10.00 **20.00**	36.00 **10.00**	40.00 **30.00**	26.47 **24.16**
Practising Professional face Greater role conflict	37.00 **25.00**	63.64 **50.00**	54.00 **65.00**	64.00 **10.00**	40.00 **40.00**	28.00 **40.00**	44.85 **38.33**
Equal in both cases	30.00 **50.00**	27.27 **5.00**	22.00 **20.00**	18.00 **70.00**	20.00 **50.00**	28.00 **30.00**	23.90 **37.5**
Can't Say	2.00 -	 -	6.00 -	8.00 -	4.00 -	4.00 -	4.41 -
It depends upon the stage of life	3.00 -	- -	- -	- -	- -	- -	0.37 -
Total	100.00 **100.00**	100.00 **100.00**	100.00 **100.00**	100.00 **100.00**	100.00 **100.00**	100.00 **100.00**	100.00 **100.00**

Professionals carring out private practice of their profession face greater conflicts in playing the dual role (44.85 and 38.33) is the opinion of the professional in largest percentages in both the studies. The reasons were that the woman has to take care of over all responsibilities of the establishment where she is practicing, including administrative matters. Whereas in employment she has to cater to the demands of her own post or part of the work. Moreover employment has financial security.

Self employment is better suited to women, than the employment, for the double role which a woman plays even now[2] (Kalbagh (ed) 1992 : 72).

The above study's finding do not match the belief of professionals of the persent study.

Professionals opining that employed professionals face greater role conflict (26.47 and 24.16) are also in good percentages. Employed professionals are bound by norms of the organisation, they are working in and have to adjust to the situation. Financial situation is also better, if the woman is having a good practice.

Percentage of women opining conflict in equal measure (23.90 and 37.50) is also sizable. The reasons given were if the organisation is not sympathetic towards the women, the staff is uncooperative; the conflicts generated are difficult to face. If the practice doesn't go well, there will be implied conflicts.

A few medical professionals made a very pertinent point that, conflicts will be more or less depending on the stage at which employment or private practice is taken up. Going for private practice is risky, especially, in the beginning; but, in later stages of the career, private practice may be more stable and rewarding. Employment is better for the beginners in the profession.

Both the studies show the same trend of opinion of the respondents. Thus, no clear picture of relationship between the two variable emerge out of both the studies. The close percentage in both the studies also show that the belief of the professionals has remained same even after a gap of 12 yrs.

Role-Conflict and the woman being the single earning member

Conflict faced by the single women who are the sole earning member in their family, are more or less in comparison to those women who have more than one earning member in the family.

77.57% professionals in 1990, and 100.00% in 2002 study, say that the conflict faced by the sole earning member are more because she has the added financial burden on her. She has to put the needs of the family before her own needs, which may generate more conflicts for her.

An earlier study has the same findings–*Economic Independence of a woman also doesnot elevate her status in the faimly even if she is the sole earner. She makes the home without feeling secure ie she is the home-maker and not the owner of the home*[3]. (Raghavan et al (ed.) 2002 : 197).

Less conflicts (6.99), and similar conflicts (3.68), was the opinion of the women in small percentages in 1990.

Profession and marriage

This is to study the opinion of the respondents regarding professionally qualified women getting married or not. That is to say, what do women who are already in profession say, about a female who has professional qualification and career to look forward to–should she enter into marital relationship, or should she forego it.

Fig : 8.4 : Opinion about professionally qualified women getting married

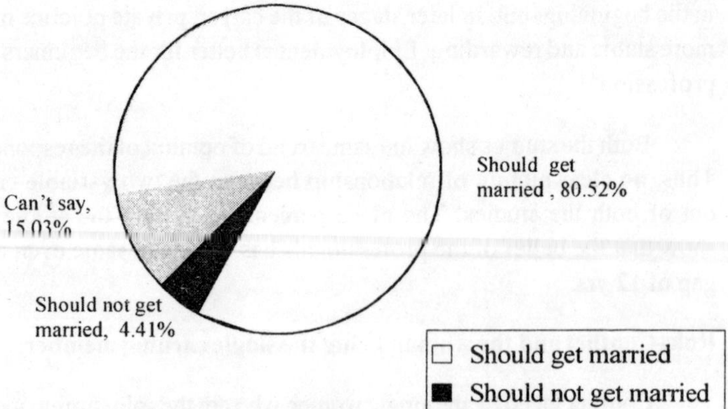

2002

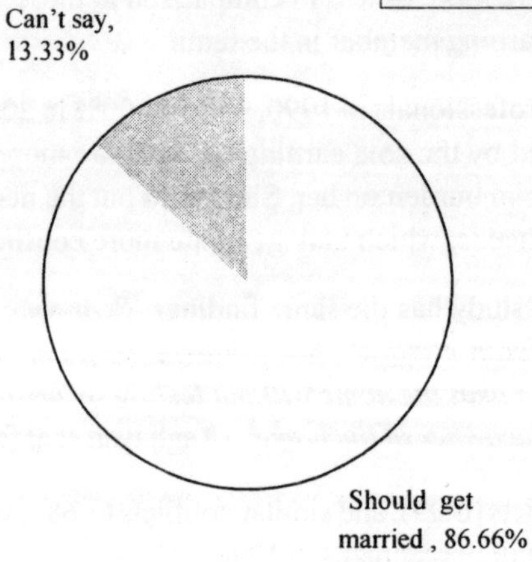

In both the studies, professionals in an overwhelming majority, are of the opinion that professionally qualified woman should get married (80.52 and 86.66). In 1990, largest percents are from teaching (84.00), followed by nursing, and engineering (82.00), medicine (80.00), social work (78.00), and law (72.00). While in 2002, largest percentages are from the professions of Social work (100.00), teaching (95.00), nursing and engineering (90.00), law (75.00) and medicine (70.00).

The next category is that of those professionals (15.00 and 13.33) who can't say about it as it depends upon the aim of the woman–law (27.00 and 25.00) and medicine (18.00 and 30.00) have this opinion in largest percentages in both the studies. Should not get married was not professed by any respondent in 2002 and in 1990 only 4.41% had this view-engineering and social work (8.00 each) nursing (4.00), teaching and medicine (2.00 each). Respondents were of the view that marriage is an important aspects of life and should not be missed out for reasons of companionship, social security and fulfillment in life.

Mahajan (1966 : 168) found among Punjab University women students in Chandigarh that, *82.2% of these students expected to fulfil both functions of marriage and career; 66.6 % even wanted to work after marriage, but only if their future husbands agreed. Only 7.6% gave preference to career, in case of a conflict*[4].

Time period devoted for professional pursuit

Table : 8.5 : Maximum time period for which the various type of professionals can remain out for work

Time period in hrs	Unmarried	Married without children	Married with small children
Less than 4 hrs	- -	-	18.38 **1.04**
4-5 hrs	1.84 **9.43**	2.21 **2.22**	64.34 **81.15**
6-7 hrs	23.16 **24.00**	41.18 **32.32**	- -
8 hrs	36.02 **30.18**	44.12 **36.36**	15.81 **14.58**
More than 8 hrs	33.08 **31.13**	12.00 **27.27**	0.37 **3.12**
Total	100.00 **100.00**	100.00 **100.00**	100.00 **100.00**

For unmarried professionals, 8 hrs jobs is favoured by the largest percentage of respondents in both the studies (36.02 and 30.18). Respondents are of the view that unmarried professionals can even work for more than 8 hrs a day (33.08 and 31.13).

For married women without children, 8 hrs job is professed by largest percentage of professionals, in both the studies (44.12 and 36.36), while 6-7 hrs jobs is professed by respondents in next largest percentage (41.18 and 32.32).

For married women with small children, in largest percentage (64.34 and 81.15), responders said that they should work only for 4-5 hours in a day, so that their house-hold chores are not neglected and they have the satisfaction of doing professional practice as well. Social workers (93.33), hold this opinion in largest percentage in 2002, while teachers (78.00) were in largest percentage in 1990. Some professionals (18.38 and 1.04) were of the opinion that married professionals with children should work for only less than 4 hours a day.

Image in other people's mind

When a person acts or behaves in a particular fashion, people around him or her, form an image of that person in context to that particular behaviour or act.

In our society women going out of home to pursue their profession in large numbers is relatively a recent phenomenon. And that too, for a male dominated profession like engineering and law. When the woman goes out for work, her working status leaves an impression on the social environment around her.

Thus, it was thought that it will be interesting to know what kind of an impression, people in general, with whom she interacts on a regular basis in society, form about her being a working professional. Positive image naturally means that people are in awe of the professional status, and negative image may reflect on the disapproval for the professional engagement of the women.

Largest percentage are of those professionals whose opinion is that they have a good image in the eyes of people in general (71.37 and 83.33). Profession wise break up runs as – medicine (77.78 and 100.00), law (81.82 and 90.00), engineering (76.0 and 100.00), teaching (82.98 and 100.00) nursing (54.0 and 15.00), and social work (62.50 and 60.00).

When the image is so-so (15.69 and 15.00) the professions having respondents from both the studies are, nursing (40.00 and 18.00), and social work (20.00 and 40.00). Law (100.00) appears only in 2002 data, and medicine (14.58), engineering (12.00) and teaching (12.16) appear in 1990 data as having so-so image.

In 2002, none of the respondents were of the opinion that their professional status generates a bad image in society, or people around her, while in 1990 (5.99) respondents professed to have a negative image because of there involvement in profession. Nursing (16.00), engineering (8.00), social work (2.50), and teaching (2.13) fall under this category.

In not bothered category 7.45% professional appear from all the 6 professions in 1990, with the highest percentage from law (18.18), followed by social work (15.00), and nursing (12.00).

Thus, it can be concluded from the statistics available from both the studies that professionals have been able to generate a good image in other peoples mind. This impression has improved over the period of time when only good image has been opined by professionals of some of the professionals like medicine, engineering and teaching. This view is supported by another study. *A significant attitudinal change towards women is evident particularly in urban areas, and a vast section belonging to the urban middle class have been acquiring an altogether new status in our society. They are the white collared, or shall I say white bloused workers of India.*[2] (Kalbagh (ed) 1992 : 172). Nursing followed by social work doesn't meet the approval of some sections of the society.

One respondent in 2002 study was of the opinion that she assess a very confused image about her being a nursing professional in the mind of people she comes across

Circumstances under which professionally qualified women should take up professional practice

It is a question which needs to be addressed that should a professionally qualified woman take up the practice of the profession for which she has acquired technical expertise in which ever circumstance she is in. What do the respondents think, that irrespective of the family norms and conditions, once the woman has studied for the profession, it should be pursued in the interest of the society and the country which has made investment in giving her technical qualification. Or practice of the profession is not obligatory on the part of the woman and it is rather circumstancial. Findings of the field data is presented here;

Table : 8.6 : Circumstances of woman by the profession of the respondent

Option	Profession						
	Medicine	**Law**	**Engineering**	**Teaching**	**Nursing**	**Social work**	**Total**
Should work in normal circumstances	72.00 -	81.82 -	78.00 -	52.00 **40.00**	76.00 **25.00**	60.00 -	68.75 **10.83**
In case of financial difficulties	12.00 -	 **5.00**	14.00 -	12.00 -	10.00 **5.00**	20.00 **25.00**	12.50 **5.83**
To pass time	8.00 -	- -	2.00 -	2.00 -	2.00 -	4.00 -	5.88 -
To avoid confrontation at home	2.00 	- -	- -	2.00 -	2.00 -	2.00 -	1.47 -
If family cooperates	2.00 -	9.09 -	2.00 -	4.00 -	8.00 -	4.00 -	3.68
If she wants to use her talent	- -	9.09 -	- -	2.00 **10.00**	2.00 -	4.00 -	2.21 **1.66**
If family life is not disturbed	6.00 -	- -	4.00 -	10.00 -	- -	2.00 -	4.04 -
Should work in all circumstances	- **80.00**	- **90.00**	- **20.00**	- **10.00**	- **60.00**	- **65.00**	- **74.16**
Depends on family circumstances	6.00 -	- -	4.00 -	10.00 **40.00**	- -	2.00 -	4.04 -
When children grow up	- **10.00**	- **5.00**	- -	- -	- -	- -	- **2.50**
If health permits	- **10.00**	- -	- -	- -	- -	- -	- **1.66**
If husband is understanding	- -	- -	- -	- -	- **10.00**	- -	**1.66**
Base	100.00 **100.00**	100.00 **100.00**	100.00 **100.00**	100.00 **100.00**	100.00 **100.00**	100.00 **100.00**	100.00 **100.00**

The data of the two studies clearly show a marked difference in the opinion of the respondents. Women have become more conscious of their professional status. In 2002 study respondents in overwhelminly large percentages, (74.16) have expressed their opinion that a professionally qualified woman should undertake the professional practice in all circumstances.

While in 1990, largest percent is of those women who professed that a woman should take up her professional practice only in normal circumstance (68.75). In 2002, this opinion was expressed by only 10.83% respondents, coming from the profession of teaching (40.00) and nursing (25.00).

Other options appearing in both the studies are in case of financial (12.50 and 5.83) difficulties and emergent situations like death of the husband.

Thus, it can be concluded that professionally qualified women of today are more pragmatic and more assertive of their professional capacities and want to exercise their right of taking up the profession for which they have spent time and money in good measure.

On the contrary, *a survey, conducted on 5000 working women in England, Scotland, West and North Ireland showed that if finances allowed, 48% of working women would choose to be a woman of leisure, 32% a home-maker and only 20% a career woman.*[6] (Times of India, June 6, 2002)

Most Suitable Profession for the female

After being in the profession for a number of years, in the opinion of the respondents, which is the best suited profession for women and girls in Indian society, where expectations from the female folk with regards to their domestic responsibilities are high and in professional field also there is cut throat competition for them. Added to this is the ambition to prove their worth in the profession.

Women have been successful in all the professions they are involved in. Large numbers are working in hospitals. Many have entered legal profession. Indian women are economists, scientists, engineers and technologists, is the begining of the new phenomenon[7]. (Devendra k. 1985 : 52)

Let us see the above statement in the light of emperical findings of the present studies.

Table : 8.7 : Respondents' opinion about the most suitable profession for girls

Most Suitable Profession	1990	Most Suitable Profession	2002
Teaching	88.01	Depends on the choice of the Individual	**28.33**
Medicine	15.44	Teaching	**42.5**
Bank and office jobs	8.82	Any part time job	**1.66**
Nursing	10.66	Nursing	**3.32**
Law	2.21	Bank/Business at home	**1.66**
Social Work	2.94	Administrative jobs	**2.50**
Depends on the choice of the individual	13.60	Creative jobs	**6.66**
Base	100.00		**100.00**

Teaching is opted as the best suited profession for women and girls, by the respondents in both the studies (88.01 and 42. 50), as the profession needs less time for professional practice. And, there are a lot of holidays and vacations given in this profession. Moreover, the timings coincide with the school timings of their children, such that the care of their children is also not a problem.

The result of field data goes with the conclusion drawn by Ranade and Ramchandran in their survey *(1970 : 62)- Teaching occupied an important place and indeed of pride as it has the advantage of a comparatively limited hours of work, good social status and enabled the women to take care of their domestic choice*[8].

Other studies also concurs with this result. *The teaching profession is considered to be respectable for a woman. And the nursing profession clearly suffers from a social stigma. But, in industrial centres, these prejudices are quickly vanishing as economic necessity compells more and more women to take to office work and nursing*[9] (Jha and Pujari (Ed.) 1996 : 180).

According to a newspaper report. (TOI, May 6, 2003) *Women are more educated and employed at a higher levels than ever before but remain largely confined to traditional pink-collar jobs. A study by the American Association of University Woman find the highest proportion of college educated working women are in teaching and nursing.*[10]

Silverstone (1980) observes that all women use contigency approach in selection of their career. To cite an eg. all over the world medicine and teaching attract more women than the other professions for they provide greater flexibility and are compatable with the image of woman as gentle and emotionally responsive and fulfiling the mother role of women.[11] (Kalbagh 1992 : 150).

Ramu (1989 : 112) is also of the view that *most of the women occupy themselves with traditional jobs like teaching, nursing and social work but there has been a gradual switch over to higher status jobs.*[12]

After teaching, respondents in next largest percentage opt for the opinion, it depends upon the choice of the individual (13.60 and 28.33) as all the professions are good for women. Devanadra's study has also reported the same finding.

Nursing and administrative jobs like IAS and Bank jobs, are also recommended by the respondents, as suitable for the women.

Opinion about their own profession

After working in their profession, what do the women professionals feel about their choice of profession. Does their experience in the profession teach them that it is not suitable for women in general, and it is more suitable for males, or do they feel that the profession suit women, and that they have a professional edge over their male counter parts. And lastly, male and female both can pursue the profession without any difficulty.

Both the studies have respondents in largest percent having the opinion that there is no difference between male and female as far as pursuing their profession (56.62 and 50.00); the highest percent are from medicine and engineering (76.00 each) in 1990, and medicine (75.00) and social work (70.00) in 2002.

Females are more suitable than males for the profession (33.82 and 33.33) is the opinion of respondents in largest percentage from the profession of teaching (56.00 and 70.00), followed by nursing (50.00 and 50.00).

Females being less suitable than males is advocated by 6.19% respondants in 1990, and 11.66% in 2002 study, with the largest percentage of respondents coming from law (36.36), followed by engineering (12.00) in 1990, and engineering (45.00), followed by law (25.00) in 2002.

Thus, it can be concluded that medicine and social work are the professions which can be taken up both by males and females, without any difference while teaching and nursing are more suitable for females; law and engineering professions are less suitable for females.

Attitude adopted by the professionals to minimum problems at home

What qualities should a working woman possess so as to minimise the number of problems she faces because of her dual role, at home and at the place of work. In other words, what is the opinion of the respondents, with regards the attitude adopted by the working women professionals, so that the problem which they face because of working at two places are reduced and tackled without much conflict and tension.

Tabel : 8.8 : Atitude adopted by a professional to reduce her conflicts

Atitude adopted by a professional	1990	**2002**
Sincere and responsible	6.25	-
Compromising and adjusting/ practical	30.15	**30.83**
Active, smart/ Swift	27.21	**29.16**
Polite, patient and humble	29.41	**45.83**
Good temperament	27.94	-
Hard working	13.97	**15.00**
Keep healthy	9.19	-
Intelligent to understand the psychology of people	6.62	-
Tolerant	15.81	-
Organised	14.00	**20.83**
Should not be egoistic & too ambitious	14.00	**9.16**
Keep two fronts separate	-	**8.33**
Base	100.00	**100.00**

Professionals in both the studies came out with a list of qualities that working women should have so as to be more adapt in handling home and work front efficiently.

Compromising and adjusting nature of the professional has been advocated by of the respondents (30.15 and 30.83) in both studies in large percentages.

She has to be active, smart and swift is the opinion of 27.21% (1990) and 29.16% (2002) women. Being polite and patient is a quality advocated by 29.41% respondents in 1990, and 45. 83% respondents in 2002.

In 1990, 13.97% and 15.00% respondents (in 2002) are of the opinion that hard work and sincerety should be a equality of the professional woman.

She has to be more organized than a housewife(14.00 and 20.83). Another suggestion for better handling of the two fronts is that women professionals should not be egoistic and too ambitious (14.00 and 9.16).

Thus, an ideal working professional is one who is compromising, practical, polite, hard working, organized and devoid of ego.

Ability of women to do all kind of jobs

It is generally felt that women cannot do all sort of jobs which the men folk do, as a routine. But, with the passage of time often, women's achievement in new and adventurous fields are also being heard. Now women are recruited in forces, women are cosmonauts, mountaineers, gliders, train drivers and even good politicians. Thus, women have entered all areas of work, all vocations and nearly all professions.

Respondents' views about women doing all kind of jobs has been presented in the following diagram.

Fig : 8.9 : Women's ability to do all sort of jobs

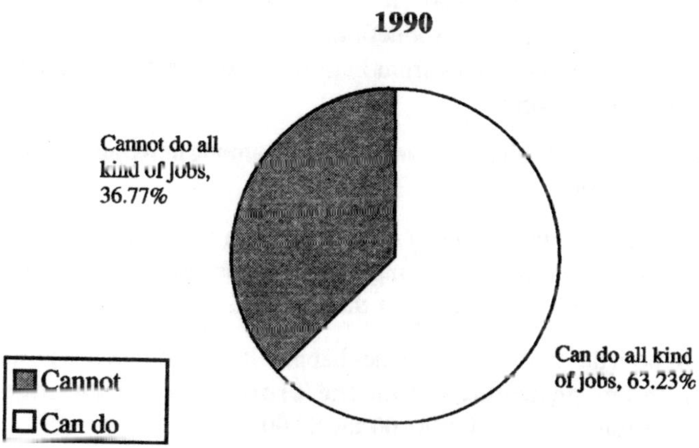

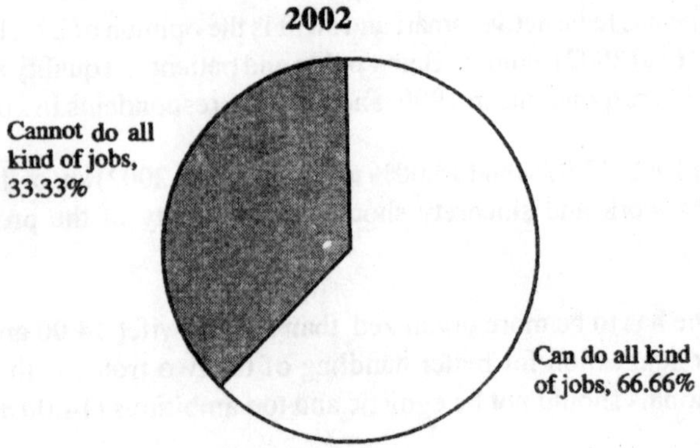

Majority, in both the studies have the opinion that women can do all kind of jobs (63.23 and 66.66). After a time gap of more than 10 years, when womens' appearance in new and unheard of professions and vocations is seen with more regularity; opinion of professionals in the city of Lucknow has not changed that sharply. Some of the studies also have the same findings.

Sood (1991 : 121) remarks–*the traditionally exclusive domain of activities for man and women have become today more common to both. There are a few areas left having masculine and feminine activities today, because of equalising effects of modern education, migration, mobility and equalitarian ideology*[13].

Opinion about what kind of jobs a women should not do, have jobs requiring excessive physical labour; police, soldiers; jobs requiring excessive touring; jobs with indefinite job-hours, and jobs in difficult circumstances. Respondents from both the studies have come out with almost the same 'don'ts'.

Opinion of the respondents towards the trend among newcomers in joining their profession

What is the trend among new entrants in the profession, do they happily join it or join it under compelling circumstances. The following is the opinion of the respondents of the two studies;

In both the studies, the females happily joint it, opinion is projected in maximum percentage from the professions of engineering (64.00 and 100.00), medicine (62.00 and 80.00).

Females join when no alternative course remains left to them social work (12.00) appear in highest percentage in 1990 and only law; (5.00), appear in the 2002 study.

Depends on circumstances have large percent of respondents from law professionals (72.73) in 1990, and nursing professionals (65.00) followed by teaching (50.00) in 2002.

Fig : 8.10 : Opinion of the respondents towards the trend among new comers in joing their profession

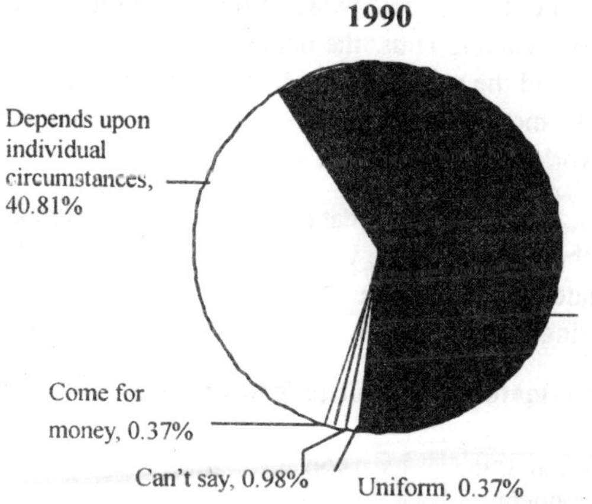

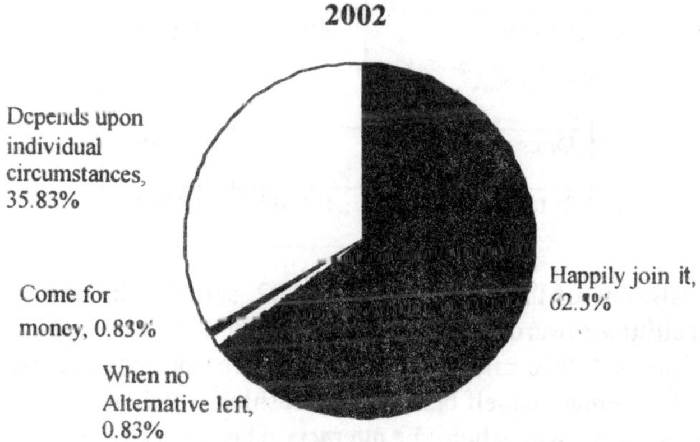

Thus, it can be observed from the field data that, medicine and engineering remains highly adored profession with girls; nursing, social work and law are circumstancial pick.

Discriminatory social altitude toward working women

When a woman decides to step out of the four-walls of the house, she infact shakes the traditional image of a woman who is supposed to remain at home and discharge her duties with in those premises.

But, in case of professionally qualified women, the admission to the professional course itself gives a signal that the woman shall be taking up the practice of the profession after completion of the course.

People around her are already aware of the possibility of adoption of the profession as a career. Thus, the acceptance of these women by the family, relatives and the society as a whole, becomes comparatively easier. But, when we move around in the society, discriminatory social altitudes towards working women is still seen at times.

It was with the idea to register what is the opinion of the respondents who at times may themselves be the victim of this malady. Do they feel that this discriminatory attitude is just or unjust ? The emperical data presents the following picture;

Table : 8.10 : Discriminatory social altitude toward working women

Opinion of the respondents	1990	**2002**
Just	4.78	-
Unjust	86.76	**69.16**
Can't Say	8.00	**14.16**
Does not exist	-	**16.66**
Total	100.00	**100.00**

Not one of the respondents in 2002, said that the discriminatory social attitude towards working women is just. In 1990, a small percent of respondents-4.78% said it is just, and the reason given is that, that at times the woman herself behaves in a fashion which arouses a negative image in people with whom she interacts. These working women leave an impression on people which becomes a perception for working women in general.

But in majority, the respondents felt it's unjust (86.76 and 69.16), and it should be removed from the society. They suggested measures which can help in removing this attitude; education of the masses, more number of women joining work force, and projection of positive image of working women in the media, which may lead to better acceptance of working women by the society.

A good percentage of respondents (8.00 and 14.16) were not able to say any thing regarding this. The percentage has increased in the second study, which is interesting to make a note of.

Another 16.66 % respondents in 2002 even stated that it does not exist now. In this context, a report which appeared in The Times of India, 13th May 2003, speaks to the contrary. *But, soon she (Justice Leila Seth) found that despite reaching the top, there was no getting away from old mind set and archaical rules, which discriminate against women.* The same news item further throw light on discrimination aganist women at work place. *This persisting discrimination against women has been highlighted in the ILO study which says, though there are more working women now than 50 years ago, they are still concentrated in lower paid and lower skilled jobs and placing women in the unskilled, lower paying wage category, and men in skilled higher wage category level of the job*[14], the report added.

The Economic Times, May 13, 2003, also reported, *Work place Discrimination Rampant Globally: ILO. Discrimination remains rampart in the workplace world wide, depriving women, ethnic and religious minorities and migrants of equal jobs or pay*[15].

The report further throws light on the fact that the most blatant type of discrimination were fading but the subtle, less visible and more insidious ones have taken their place.

Women are the most common targets of discrimination, suffering from both – the glass ceiling, preventing their advancement and significant "pay gaps" even where their educational level was equal to that of men, the ILO report said.

Women who are secondary in the family and who play supportive, sustaining and conflict resolving roles are expected to play the same role in the work setting also[16]. (Kalbagh 1992 : 151)

But Tara Ali Baig in India's Women Power writes" extracts of studies, articles and research underline the fact that Asian and Africa women strongly hold different values to their sister in many northern and western societies (but)......... they feel (that) they feel less discrimination in modern career situations, for instance then their counter parts in west. Further more, Asian female stereotypes is without the sharp dichotomy between male and female that has led to militant female movements in recent times[17]. (Devendra Kiran 1985 : 12)

Working, a Human Right issue

In times of today every body talks of human rights. Putting a kind of restriction on a person's way of thinking and acting especially if it is not antisocial, amounts to violation of his/ her human right.

It was thought appropriate to include the issue of violation of human rights in the assessment of respondent's views in 2002; if a professionally qualified woman is not allowed to take her profession by her family.

Majority (77.00%) of the respondents are of the view that it amounts to violation of human rights, if a professionally qualified woman is not allowed to take up her professional pursuit. It is observed in an analysis of the field data that more technical and high status the profession, higher is the percent of respondents opining the above view; engineering (100.00), law (95.00), medicine (80.00), teaching and social work (70.00 each) and nursing (50.00).

Another 7.50% of the respondents had nothing to say on this; (medicine-20.00 nursing-15.00 and teaching-10.00) while another 7.50% said it depends on the circumstance of the woman, if not letting her take up her profession is a violation of human rights, or it is justified (nursing-35.00 and teaching 10.00). Yet another 7.50% respondents were of the view that it not violation of the human right (social workers-30.00, teaching-10.00 and Laws 5.00).

Thus, the issue of violation of human rights, by not letting a professionally qualified woman take up her professional pratice, form the majority opinion. Professionals from different professionals have reasons of their own for not going by the majority which includes indecisiveness in the matter, calling it just and the situation deciding the issue of violation or not.

References

1. Reddy, C.R. : Changing Status of Educated Working Woman, B.R. Publishing Corp. Delhi (1986 , p. 15).
2. Kalbagh, C. (ed) : Women in Enterprise and Profession, Discovery Publishing House, New Delhi (1992 , p. 72).
3. Raghvan, Veera, Singh , Shalini and Khandewal, Kanika (ed) : The Child in New Millenem, Mosaic Books New Delhi (2002 , p. 197).
4. Mahajan, A. : Women's two roles. A Study of Role Conflict. The Indian Journal of Social Work : Vol. XX VI 4 (1966 p. 168).
5. Kalbagh, C. (ed) : Women in Enterprise and Profession, Discovery Publishing House, New Delhi (1992 , p.1 72).
6. Times of India : Not many taker of super model tag, June 6, 2002.
7. Devendra, K. : Status and Profession of Women of India, Vikas Publishing House, Ghaziabad (1985 : pg. 52).
8. Ranade and Ram Chandran : Women and Employment (TISS Study) (1970, p. 62).
9. Jha and Pujari (ed) : Indian Woman Today, Vol. 3, Kanishika Pubulications, New Delhi (1996 , p. 180).
10. Times of India, May 6, 2003 : Woman Moving up but in traditional jobs.
11. Kalbagh, C. (ed) : Women in Enterprise and Profession, Discovery Publishing House, New Delhi (1992, p. 150).
12. Ramu, G.N. : Woman Work and Marriage in Urban India, Sage Publication, New Delhi, New Bury park/London (1989, p. 112).
13. Sood, R. : Changing Status and Adjustment of Women, Mahak Publication Pvt. Ltd, Jaipur/Delhi (1991, p. 121).
14. Times of India : Discrimination against woman, May 13, 2003.
15. The Economics Times : Work Place Discrimination rampant globally : ILO, May 13, 2003.
16. Kalbagh, C. (ed) : Women in Enterprises and Profession, Discovery Publishing House. New Delhi (1992 , p. 151).
17. Devendra, K. : Status and Profession of Women of India, Vikas Publishing House, Ghaziabad (1985, p. 12).

CHAPTER 9

MAJOR FINDINGS

After Independence, because of the constitutional provisions and allied legislations related to the equality of men and women, with respect to the exercise of their freedoms and fundamental rights, and also due to the impact of the west, Indian working women have become a force to reckon with in the labour market. Their presence has become sizeable not only in pink-collar jobs, but also in blue and white collared jobs.

For the purpose of this study, practising women professionals from six specialized fields viz., medicine, law, engineering, teaching, nursing, and social work, were chosen. The sample size was 272, in the first study (undertaken for the Ph D dissertation) in 1990, and the sample size was 120, in the second study, undertaken to study and assess the decadal shifts, transformations and changes discernible, if any, in 2002.

Fifty professionals from each of the six professions were decided upon, but due to the paucity of 50 lady lawyers, during the first study, the sample size came down to 272, as only 22 lady lawyers were found practicing in Lucknow City.

For the second study, the sample size was 120, with 20 respondents interviewed, from each of the six professions, viz., medicine, law, engineering, teaching, nursing, and social work.

The working women professionals in both the studies were in their thirties. Early 30's in the 1990 study (at an average age of 34.59 years), and in their late 30's in the 2002 study (at an average age of 37.50 years).

In 1990, nurses were, on an average, the oldest respondents at 38.60 years, while **social workers average as the oldest respondents, in the 2002 study,** at 41 years. Chi square test when applied to both the data shows a significant relationship between the two variables of profession and age of the respondents in both the studies.

Most of the respondents in both the samples are married (65.44 percent of the respondents in the 1990 study, and 55.00 percent in the 2002 study). The largest percentage of married respondents come from the field of medicine (82.00) in the 1990 study, while the field of engineering threw up the largest percentage of married respondents (90.00), in the 2002 study. The profession and marital status bear no relationship in the 1990 study, but in the 2002 study, they show a significant relationship when subjected to chi-square test.

A majority of the respondents are Hindu (75.37 in 1990, and 80.83 in 2002); maximum percent from law (90.91) and engineering (90.00) in 1990, and law and medicine (95.00 each) in 2002. **The percentage of Muslim women increased** from 5.88% to 7.50%, with a sizable percent from the teaching profession (40.00), in 2002. On the other hand, **the percentage of Christian women decreased** from 12.87% in 1990, to 5.00% in 2002. **Representation of Sikh women remained almost same,** at 3.31 % and 3.33%, while the percentage of Jain respondents also showed an increase (from 2.57% in 1990, to 3.33% in 2002). Religion and profession appear to have a mutual dependence, as becomes apparent, when X^2 test is applied on both the data.

The respondents are predominantly from nuclear families (52.71% in 1990, and 54.16% in 2002). Chi-square test show a significant relationship between the type of family, and the profession of the women in 2002, while no such significant relationship is discernible, in the 1990 study.

Kayastha women constituted the **largest percentage** (28.78), in the **1990 study,** while the **Brahmin women** respondents were in **majority** (at 29.89), among the Hindu respondents in the **2002 study.**

Average number of children for the total sample in 1990 was 1.83, which came down to 1.20 per respondent, in 2002. Social workers at 2.18, had the maximum number of children, per head in 1990, while teachers at an average of 1.50, lead the tally in 2002. Chi square test shows no dependence of the two variables in 1990 and dependence in 2002 data.

In both the studies, the largest percentages of women have children between the age group of 7-14 years (33.33% in 1990, and 40.38% in 2002). This is followed by respondents with children in the age group of 3-6 years (29.28 % in 1990) and respondents with children of 14 years and above (35.44% in 2002).

Period of service is an important determinant in making the working woman and the family members adjust to the demands of the situation. It is logical to think that, with the passage of time, adjustment of the working woman to her routine and its demands becomes better. **A majority of the respondents have put in more than 5 years of service** (71.69% in 1990, and 56.66% in 2002). A period of 5 years may be considered as an optimal time frame in any situation - with or without children, young or older children, within which adjustment to all problems are thrashed out and the working woman settles into a grove.

Respondents with service period ranging from 1-3 years have increased in 2002 (26.66), up from 1990 (10.66). Thus, the average period of service (11.36 years to 6.9 years), has also come down in most of the professions except in the case of engineering. Chi-square test shows a significant relationship between the variables of period of service and the profession of the respondent.

Monthly income of the working women also becomes an added allurement for the family. Being professionally qualified, they do bring in a good salary packet, the addition of which leads to better amenities for the whole of the family. **Monthly income of the respondents has shown a phenomenal rise from 1990 to 2002,** mainly because of massive pay revision in the intermittent period. **The largest percentage (37.50) of professionals in the 2002 study, are earning Rs. 10,000/- or more,** and another good percentage (28.33), is earning between 5-10 thousand rupees, per month. In contrast, **the monthly income of the largest percentage (at 67.27%) ,of respondents in 1990 was below Rs. 2000** followed by 27.21% percent women, earning between Rs. (2001 – 5000).

The average income of respondents in 1990 was Rs. 2287.68, while in 2002 the average income of the total sample is Rs. 11,250.00. Doctors had the highest average income in both the studies (Rs. 3,585.00 in 1990, and Rs. 21,750.00 in 2002). Chi square test shows a significant relationship in both the studies. This is supported by the field data also.

When enquired about the **consideration for choosing their profession,** respondents saying that **it was their personal interest in the profession, constituted the largest segments, in both the studies** (54.78% in 1990, and 57.66% in 2002); respondents from the field of medicine (88.00), constituted the highest percent in this category in 1990, while professionals, from the field of social works (65.00), were the largest votaries in 2002. Empirical data shows that the choice of profession and religion followed by the respondents has no relation.

The majority of respondent were self–motivated in the choice of their profession (50.73% in 1990, and 52.50% in 2002). **Fathers** were the motivating factors of the respondents in the choice of their profession for 30.15 % respondents in **1990**, and for 25.00 % respondents in 2002; **mothers** as the motivating factors were 19.85 % in 1990, and 9.06 % in **2002.**

A majority of women started practising the profession as soon as they attained their professional qualification, and when they were still unmarried (63.97 and 83.33).* The percentage increase in the latter study shows that women no longer wait before taking a plunge into their profession, and marriage is also delayed until the qualification is attained. It has also been observed and recorded that when practice is taken up after marriage, the women had been studying the course at that time, and there was no time lapse between the completion of the educational qualification and in starting of the practice.

Application of chi square test on the data shows a significant relationship between the stage of adoption (before marriage/after marriage) and the profession of the respondent.

In 1990 the main reason for taking up of professional practice by the working women professionals was, to avoid wastage of professional talent (69.85). In both studies, respondents in large numbers (49.63 and 47.80), also said that it was a desire to be free from dependence which made them go for practice of their profession. **The above is the most widely professed reason in the 2002 study, which demonstrates that, the women of 21st century strongly desire economic independence, over any other reason for working.**

The woman of today is **self–motivated, in taking up a job as a professional** (61.40 and 62.50) and this situation stands, irrespective of the profession she pursues. When decision-making mechanism in the family was studied, **it was found that the woman was a part of the decision–making, in a majority of cases, in both the studies** (72.06% in 1990, and 74.16% in 2002). Clearly, by virtue of education, being an earning member and better exposed to the realities of the outside world, a woman is given

* Figures in parenthesis show comparison of two studies.

due importance by the family, and is an intrinsic part of the decision–making corps in the family.

On the other hand, it may be the assertiveness of the female professional, which has made her an integral part of decision making, in the family.

When the variable was studied with regards to the type of family she comes from, **in 1990 it was the woman herself who was taking decision in the family, irrespective of the nature of the family** – in a joint family (32.31), and in a nuclear family (39.44). But, in **2002 it is the woman herself in nuclear family (50.76) who is taking major decisions, while joint decision making prevails in joint families** (61.81), of which she is again a party to.

On studing the variable of persons providing help in household chores & their extent of help, it is seen that the working professional is much helped by her husband in most cases. The effect of time on this variable has remained unchanged between 1990-2002. The next in the category of helpers is the mother who also provide much help in both the studies.

When **incidences of role-conflict** were studied, it was found that in the 1990 study, most of the respondents received understanding response (59.56) from their family members when they were unable to attend to their family duties, in wake of their employment. **In 2002, the reaction is stated to be favourable (63.33). Only a small percent of women report of unfavourable reaction from the family, in the aforesaid circumstances (11.76 and 9.16) in both the studies; the largest percentage come from the profession of nursing (18.00 and 30.00) in both the studies.**

While medical professionals (90.00) receive a favourable response in largest percentage in 2002, law professionals (81.82) report of understanding response in the largest percentage, in 1990.

Analyzing the empirical data, it can be said that the **families of medical and law professionals are most receptive to the demands of the professional. In contrast, the nursing professionals are more at the receiving end of unfavourable reactions, when unable to attend to their family duties because of pressing professional demands.**

When the reaction of the family was studied against the type of family the woman comes from, it was found in **both the studies, that in joint families, the largest percentage of women received understanding attitude (50.77) in 1990, and favourable reaction (69.09) in 2002. While**

those living in nuclear families also show the same trend - understanding attitude (67.61) in 1990, and favourable reaction (58.46), in 2002.

But when the pattern of women reporting **unfavourable reaction** is analyzed, it was found that **women from nuclear families (15.49) constituted a majority in 1990, while in 2002, it was the turn of women from joint families (10.90) to receive the maximum counts of unfavourable attitude,** from their family members.

Chi square results on 1990 data show a significant relationship which is not supported by field data, but non–significant relationship on 2002 data, is supported by the field data.

When reaction of the family was studied in light of the religion of the respondents, it was found that the trend of no relationship prevailed. **A majority of women from different religions received understanding attitude in 1990 and favourable reaction in 2002.**

Professionals receiving **unfavourable reaction were found in all religions in 1990, while in 2002,** it was reported only by the **Hindu and Jain professionals. But Jain professionals, in both the studies** (28.00 in 1990, and 25.00 in 2002) **face unfavourable reaction from their family member** in larger percentages, **making them most prone to the incidents of role conflict.**

All the respondents who report of unfavourable reaction from the family when unable to take proper care of the family because of their professional pursuit report of favourable attitude toward their professional pursuits in 2002 while in 1990, 50.00% received favourable attitude, 28.13% reported of unfavourable attitude, while 21.87 % also reported of indifferent attitude of their family towards their going out for work.

When it was enquired from the respondents if the **family life, generally expected of a woman, is affected by her going out for work, a majority of women in both the studies said that their family life was not affected** (56.00 and 70.00).

When **reflectors of role conflict** were studied, it was found that **irrespective of the profession, religion or caste that she comes from, a professionally qualified woman gets favourable attitude** of her family members towards her professional pursuit. Field data show that **favourable attitude does not change by the number of children she has, or their age group nor even the period of service she has put in.**

Professionals reported unfavourable attitude in small percentages, mainly from the profession of engineering and nursing, in 1990. This further diminished in the **2002 study,** and only a small percent of professionals from the **field of medicine reported** of unfavourable attitude.

Sikh women face it the most (22.22) in the 1990 study, and Hindu Kayastha women (7.70) in 2002; both the categories have one child in both the studies and the age group of their children is (3 – 6) years. The women were in service for more than five years in both the studies.

Promila Kapur's study (1970) shows that the attitude of the husband, so far as wife's employment is concerned, is either favourably disposed, or is neutral. This observation tallies with these two studies too – the working women professionals receive favourable attitude irrespective of the type of family they may come from.

The other high light of the studies is that, in **both the studies, all the SC and OBC respondents see favourable attitude of their family towards their professional pursuit.**

In both the studies, professionals get much help from their family members in performing their house-hold jobs (57.7 and 45.85) – engineers receive it in the maximum, at 74.00% in 1990, and 70.00% teachers report of it in the 2002 study.

Professionals receiving no help have reduced in 2002. Nurses (32.00) and social workers (30.00) are the worst sufferers in the first and second study respectively. Application of chi-square test shows that the two variables, i.e., the extent of help provided to a working woman at home, and the profession, which she is pursuing, show a positive significance in both the studies.

In 1990 study much help is also received irrespective of the type of family she comes from. But, a professional coming from a **joint family,** receives more help, in much **larger percentages** (71.54 and 69.09) – while professionals living in **nuclear families receive lesser help** (45.09 and 26.15). In 2002 much help category has the lowest percentage. Chi-square testifies the dependence of the two variables viz., the extent of help and type of family, which is supported by the field data also.

When the variable of degree of interest the family shown in the promotion of her career was studied against other variables, like the profession of the female, her religion and the caste, it is found that a

majority say their family is keen to see them getting promotions (34.00 and 50.00). **Engineers command the maximum percentages in both studies** (54.00 and 85.00). Very keen interest is shown by the families of lawyers (54.55) in 1990 and the families of doctors (50.00) in 2002.

Unhelpful attitude is borne by nurses (6.00) in largest percentage, in 1990. In 2002, women saying that their family members are not unhelpful but do no help in any way either, come from the profession of teaching (50.00), in the largest percentage. Chi–square test shows that in 1990 there is no dependence of the two variables, but in the 2002 study, the data shows high dependence, which does not get much support from the empirical data.

When degree of interest was studied with reference to religion, it was found that in 1990, professionals in **majority of cases reported of keen or very keen interest of their family members, irrespective of their religion; while unhelpful attitude was faced only by the Hindu (2.43) and the Christian (5.71) professionals, in small percentages.**

In 2002 all the professionals, barring the Jains, reported to have seen keen and very keen interest in promotion of their career. All the Christian professionals (100.00) professed to have seen their family showing keen interest in the promotion of their career, while all the Jain professional (100.00) reported not-helpful attitude of their family towards their career prospects. In fact, a sizeable percent from the Hindu community (21.64), Muslim (33.33), and Sikh (15.00) also report of their families being not helpful but not unhelpful.

When caste of the respondents is studied for the **degree of interest, very keen interest is seen by SC/OBC women** (75.00) in **both the studies; not helpful attitude is assessed by professionals, from all the castes, in almost the same measure** - ranging from 25.00 % (Khatris) to 16.66% (SC/OBC) in **2002, and the Khatris (8.00) face unhelpful** attitude in the largest percentage in 1990.

Next is the **supposition that if she is not working** what is her assessment about her relationship with other people at home (excluding the husband) and with the husband, in case of married respondents.

With other people at home, the 1990 data says it would have been the same (48.44), **while the 2002 data has professionals reporting different relationships as the highest percentage** (52.50). Teachers (58.00) and social workers (56.00) are in support of the same relationship (1990 study) – doctors (75.00) and engineers (70.00) foresee a different relationship (2002 study). **Nurses (66.67) in highest percentage said that their relationship would have been different in the 1990 study, while in the 2002 study,** 70.00% **nurses say that their relationship with people at home would have been same.**

In both the studies, the majority of women are of the view that relationship when different would be more strained (58.89 and 54.65). **No financial help** (37.74) **and more time for confrontation** (33.96) are the reasons give in **1990.** In **2002** the reason cited is **frustration because of not being able to use the professional qualification** (42.62) – a reflection on the importance of putting their education to use, over any other considerations in today's time.

Thus working of women was guided by financial gains when the earlier study was conducted while at the time of latter study it is frustration which guide relationship.

Again, in case of **relationship with the husband if not working,** a **majority of the respondents in 1990 said it would remain same** (49.44), **while in 2002 it changed to different** (54.54%). Interestingly among those who foresee a different relationship in both the studies, a **majority of the respondents are of the view it would be more strained** (60.00 and 75.00). No financial help to the family (law -100.00 , nursing 76.92), and frustration on the part of the professionals for not being able to use their qualification (medicine 100.00 and teaching 100.00) were the reasons cited respectively, in the two studies.

When the same variable is seen in the back–drop of the type of family from which the women come, it was found that **irrespective of the type of family, a majority of the respondents in the 1990 study were of the view that their relationship with other people at home would remain the same** (joint family 51.63 and nuclear family 43.69). **In 2002, a majority of the respondents professed that it will be different irrespective of the type of family** (joint family 56.37 and 49.24 from nuclear family).

Amongst those who professed a different relationship, women from joint families in both the studies say that there will be a strained relationship (68.00 in the 1990 study and 64.51 in the 2002 study), while those living in nuclear families said in 1990 that it'll be more strained (60.00) because the demands of the children may not be met.

So, it may be said that in the 1990s, some 10-12 years ago, financial aspect of a working women professional was the motivating force to launch her into a professional career, while in 2002, it is the right to work and striving hard for it with a competitive spirit, has been the main motivating force for taking up any professional career.

Chi-square test when applied on both the data show no dependence of the two variables, which is supported by the empirical data as well.

The trend remains the same when the relationship if not working is seen in reference to the husband of the married respondents. **Majority of them say the same, from both type of families** (Joint – 52.27% and nuclear – 45.65%) in 1990, **while in 2002 it is different** (57.14% from joint families and 51.11% nuclear families). Thus professional pursuit if not taken up, has direct implications on marital accord in contempory time.

Interesting comparisons can be seen in case of **women reporting of different relationship** – it is professed to be **more strained irrespective of the type of family and irrespective of the time frame of the two studies.** This result is supported by the application of the chi-square test also. In both the studies, it shows no association between the two variable – more strained joint family (73.08 and 58.34), more strained and nuclear family (61.11 and 78.26).

The same variable (relationship with people if not in professional practice) when matched with the religion of the respondent, yields some interesting results – **in 1990, a majority of Hindu** (51.56), **Jain** (60.00), **and Muslim** (50.00) **women said that their relationship with other people will remain the same** whether they are in the profession or not. It is only the **Christian women** (66.66), **who voice this opinion, in majority, in 2002.**

While different relationship was seen by Sikh (62.50) and Christian (45.71) **respondents in 1990, in 2002 all professional in majority, except the Christian respondents say it would be different. Only the Muslim women in the 1990 study** (80.00), **assess their relationship with people at home to be cordial.**

Women from all the other religions in both the studies see a more strained relationship (when different) with the husband. In 2002 all the Sikh and Christian women (100.00 each) **said that their relationship would remain same irrespective of their working or non-working status. In 1990, the Hindu** (54.07) **and Muslim** (54.55) **respondents said this in largest majority.**

The women foreseeing a different relationship feel it will be more strained (75.00 in 2002) – Jain (100.00), Muslim (100.00), and Hindu (68.92). In 1990 too, more percentages of women saying different relationship believed it would deteriorate (58.06), if they are not working – Christian (90.00) and Hindu (57.14) respondents show very high percentages. Only Jain professionals (100.00) in the different category, claimed that their relationship would be more cordial.

Thus, we see that religion has no major impact on relationship with their husbands had they not been working, and data from both the studies show this clearly.

A majority of women in both the studies (60.00 and 60.00) **look for no change in their home environment to make their working at the two places easier,** reflecting their contentment with the present situation.

In 1990, doctors and engineers (24.00 and 14.00 respectively), look for better servants, while in 2002, engineers and nurses (both 100.00), look for more co-operation from their family members. These are from among those who want some change or more facilities for a better environment at home.

A majority of women in both the studies look forward to changes in work environment, which will make their working easier (70.59% in 1990 study, and 78.33% in 2002 study).

Both the studies have women asking for more cooperation from people at the work place (16.91 and 28.72). At 26.00% each doctors and nurses in 1990, and 55.00 % engineers, 40.00 % doctors, and 35.00 % lawyers have asked for specific changes at the work place, in 2002.

In 1990 a few of the changes desired were – reduced duty hours (engineers – 58.00 and social workers – 24.00); **adequate staff, equipment and funds** (nurses – 48.00 and doctors – 34.00).

While, **in the 2002 study, changes desired are basically to provide more opportunity for their professional talent to proliferate and those related to job satisfaction,** like changes in infrastructure, faster promotion, decentralization of responsibilities, more resources and autonomy at the work place.

It can be concluded that the professionals, at large, reflect that the work places may be a potent place where forces may emanate leading to generation of role conflict in the individual.

When required to stay beyond the prescribed hours of work a good majority (62.50 and 75.00) **inform at home,** and if they are not able to inform about this, in most of the cases people at home get worried (59.93 and 82.22).

If there is **some unpleasantness at home, a majority of the respondents in 1990 reported that there used to be no change in their behaviour at the place of work** (53.68) – teachers (74.00) and lawyers (72.73) said in high percentage. **In the 2002 study, nurses** (70.00) **and lawyers** (60.00) **reported of no change in behaviour, in the largest percentages.** Getting irritated (18.38 and 13.33), tensed or stressed (10.29 and 18.33), and becoming quiet and depressed (11.76 and 11.00) are the commonly seen changes in the two studies.

When inquired about their **female status being helpful for their profession or not, in the 2002 study, 56.66% respondents vouched that it was not helpful in any way, while 45.22 % respondents held the same view in the 1990 study. Female status is seen to be more helpful in case of professions like medicine and nursing where the patients are mainly female.** Also, in case of professions like teaching, nursing and social work where the professional is required to be tender, affectionate, caring, compassionate, understanding and patient, obviously, the female status has its own dividends.

When we look into the **causes of role-conflict** we find that it can be divided into three broad conflict generating areas, viz., family causes, organizational causes and societal causes.

Overwhelming majority of professionals in both the studies said that their family has a favourable attitude towards their purshing the career.

When relation between family and professional responsibilities - whether the two type of responsibilities are in conflict, complementary, or neither – was examined, **it was found that both the studies have women reporting of the complementary nature of the two types of responsibilities in large percentage** (41.55 and 54.16). Only a small number of respondents said that the two types of responsibilities are in conflict (11.03 in 1990, and 8.23 in 2002).

Complementarity of the two responsibilities is opined in largest percentages by 54.55% of lawyers in 1990, while 85.00 % of engineers hold this view, in 2002. Conflicting nature of the two types of

responsibilities was reported in the largest percentage by medical and engineering professionals (18.00 each), **in 1990, and by medical professionals** (20.00) **in 2002.**

When nature of relationship between family and professional responsibilities was studied against the type of family the woman comes from, it was found that **women from joint family report of neither conflicting nor complementing nature of relationships** (50.00 in 1990, and 52.72 in 2002). **Professionals from nuclear families report of complementary nature of relationship in the largest percentages** (47.78 in 1990, and 69.23 in 2002).

When **conflicting relationship** was analyzed, it was found that the percentage of women from **nuclear families was more in 1990** (14.08), **while the percentage in 2002 was more from joint family** (9.09) **showing the change in trend over a period of time.**

When the nature of relationship was seen with regards to the marital status of the woman, it is seen that **divorced and widowed professionals** (100.00 each) **find it complementing in 2002, while widows** (68.75) **and separated** (66.67) **women professionals found the two complementing, in largest percentages in 1990. It is only the married women in both the studies, who report of conflicting nature of relationship of the two responsibilities, in both the studies** (14.08% in 1990, and 13.68% in 2002).

When the decision–making authority includes the professional herself or her husband or it's joint mechanism, **the incidence of complementing each other's responsibilities is high. When father/ mother or the in-laws are making decisions, the reported relationship is neither complementary nor conflicting.**

The empirical data shows that the **nature of relationship remains predominantly complementary in both the studies, when the number of children increase.** The trend is clearer in the 1990 data. Interestingly, when the women report of no children, then too the percentage of complementary relationship is very high (72.72) in the 2002 study.

When the professionals have more than three children, the relationship is complementary in the largest percentages, in both the studies (71.43 in 1990, and 100.00 in 2002). The chi-square test on the 1990 data show a significant relationship, while the test on 2002 data shows no significant relationship. The results are concurrent with the field data.

When monthly income of the respondents was analyzed with regards to the nature of relationship between professional and domestic responsibilities, it is seen that **when the income is high, the nature of relationship in complementary in large percentages.** The trend is clearer in the 2002 study's data as 1990 has some variations. When the income is below rupees 2000 and between rupees 2-5 thousand, then the nature of relationship reported by the majority is neither conflicting nor complementary (39.4% and 45.95% respectively, for the two categories).

Conflicting relationship, although reported in small percentages, has the largest percentage when income group is (2-5) thousand rupees, 12.16% in 1990, and when the income is above 10,000.00%, it is 13.33% in the 2002 study.

In 1990 a majority of the professionals were of the view that their family would have neither welcomed nor condemned their not taking up their profession (54.78). In 2002 a majority (51.66) **of the sample size said that their families would have condemned their not being in professional practice** – engineers at 85.00% top this opinion chart in 2002, while in 1990, social workers (78.00) professed a neutral reaction of their family as the largest percentage group.

Sitting at home would have been welcomed in case of nurses (22.00) **in 1990, and by the doctors' families** (20.00) **in 2002 study.** The overall percentage of welcomed category has come down in 2002 as the families now understand that practising of the profession by their daughter or daughter-in-law is not only financially profitable to them, but also leads to a better status in society.

When reaction of the family if professional practice is not taken up was studied against other variables like attitude of family towards their working, **it is found that in both the studies females report of getting favourable attitude and condemning reaction** (82.93 and 95.08) in great majority. Chi square test shows dependency in 1990 data and not being dependent in case of 2002 study, which is supported by the field data analysis.

Nature of relationship between domestic and professional responsibilities, when related to reaction of the family if not working, show professionals in largest percentages reporting complementary relationship and favourable attitude (57.32 and 67.74). **While in conflict and welcomed reaction in largest percentages in 1990 (23.68), and in**

conflict and condemned reaction in 2002 (9.67) . Chi square test on 1990 and 2002 data show that both the variables are related. But field data while supporting the result of 1990, does not go with 2002 results.

While conflicting relationship is small in 1990 data, when the husband takes decisions (5.00). **In 2002, when husband is the decision maker the percentage is appreciable** (33.33).

This points to the fact that the conflict in both type of responsibilities may have a bearing when the decision-maker is the husband, and also that today's woman professional is more assertive.

When the organizational causes were probed, the first thing that comes to the mind is the incidence of undue liberties being taken by people at the place of work. **A majority of respondents in both the studies have reported of facing no incidence of undue liberties being taken with them at the work place** (75.00 and 85.33).

Where **incidents of undue liberty being taken of are accepted** (19.12% in 1990 and 10.83% in 2002), **the maximum percent of professional are from engineering profession** (52.00) **in 1990, and law professionals** (20.00) **in 2002. Higher up officials, or superiors are the most likely people trying to take undue liberties** (42.31in 1990 and 61.53 in 2002) **in both the studies**, but **in 1990 the a majority of the working women professional** (48.08) **have also reported about their colleagues' involvement in such conduct.**

When the analysis of data was done with regards to the job satisfaction as a professional, it was found that a **majority of the respondents** (59.19 and 65.83) **in both the studies are satisfied with the work they are currently engaged in.** The largest percent are from law (90.91) in 1990, and from the profession of teaching (90.00) in the 2002 study. **None of the engineering professionals (100.00) in 2002 said that they are wholly satisfied,** while in 1990 also, the percent of respondents not wholly satisfied with their job was the highest from the engineering profession (66.00). The **dissatisfied category has only doctors, in both the studies** (4.00 and 10.00).

Next is the assesment of **effects of role conflict.** It is generally seen that role–conflict has its own deleterious ramifications and may lead to various maladaptive consequences upon the working woman professional unless it is addressed squarely, and modifications effected.

Role conflict may also affect the persons who are associated with her, both at home and at her place of work – equally, it leaves its mark upon the nature, quality and efficiency of her performance at both these places.

As women remain the sole charge de affairs of the household chores, once her performance at home suffers, conflict is inevitable. The empirical data – **the women professionals in both the studies, in majority, speak of no ill effect of their professional pursuit upon their house hold chores** (54.04 and 72.50). The rise in percentage is appreciable, between 1990 and 2002, showing better management of family affairs and adaptability of the family members and the working woman professional now. Lawyers (72.73) and teachers (68.00) in 1990, and lawyers and nurses (90.00 of each) and social workers (80.00) in 2002, are the highest votaries of this view.

Kapur 1974 says that addition of roles of a working women to the set of her traditional roles of a wife and mother does create difficult situation and does produce conflict and tension within her on account of her drive to carry out her dual responsibilities at home and work place efficiently. The present study do concur with this, thus pointing out on the change of scene.

Care of children (46.40 and 75.75) **tops the list of the neglected chores. Women professionals in medicine and social work confess to this, in both the studies.**

Another neglected area (chores) is the general upkeep and management of the house, leading to wastages. Once again, professionals from the field of medicine and social work are the largest subscribers to this malady, in both the studies.

The analysis of the data from the two studies, reveals that the working women professionals are now able to manage the home-front in a better way, the reasons being – more help and cooperation from the family members and better facilities and amenities available at home, than before.

Application of chi square test (on the data from both the studies) shows a significant relation between the household responsibilities and profession of the woman.

When house hold duties affected or not is studied in relation to the type of family, in 1990 a greater percent of working **women professionals saying that their household duties are affected, came from nuclear families** (57.04), **while in 2002, it is the working women professionals coming from joint families** (32.12), who say that their household responsibilities are neglected. Application of chi-square test shows a significant relationship in 1990 and a non-significant relationship in 2002.

Household responsibilities being neglected when seen against the age group of children of the respondents, show higher percentages in the affected category in 1990 (53.60), **and not affected in 2002** (50.62), but the difference in percentage of the two categories is very small in 2002. **When affected category in household work is seen, it shows that in both the studies, it is the category with infants up to 2 years, which is in maximum percentages** (73.68 and 100.00). On applying X^2 test to both the data, dependence of the two variables results in 2002, while no dependence is the 1990 revelation.

When asked, **if she was not in her professional practice** does the working woman professional think that her **family affairs would have been better managed, it was in the negative in both the studies** (58.45 and 83.33). **There is a phenomenal rise in the percent of respondents who shot down this assertion, in the second study – this is again indicative of the growing assertiveness, confidence and will of the women to take up their professional practice, as a natural adjunct to their other gender specific roles.** The percentages from all the professions are very high in 2002, ranging from 80.00% (social works) to 100.00 %, (engineering) except in the profession of medicine.

In 1990, the profession of law (72.73) and nursing (72.00) show the highest percentages. The category of aye for this assertion has the professionals from the fields of medicine (46.00 and 40.00) and social work (42.00 and 20.00), showing very high percent of approbation with this assertion in both the studies – engineers with 50.00 % ayes, were high in the charts, in 1990.

When attitude of family members towards professional pursuit and management of family affairs if not working, were studied in relation to each other, it was found that **when the assessment is that family affairs would have been better managed, then women in majority, face unfavourable altitude of the family towards their professional practice** (52.94 in 1990, and 100.00 in the 2002 study).

On the other hand, **the no effect category encounters favourable attitude in higher percents** (59.01 in 1990, and 83.50 in 2002). On application of chi-square test, no dependence between the variables has been found for the 1990 data, while when applied on the 2002 one, it shows high dependence – this is supported by the field data.

When number of children of the respondents was seen in the back drop of management of family affairs if not working, it was found in both the studies that **as number the of children increases, the percent of professionals responding, would have been better managed, decreases.** On the other hand, when no effect is reported, with increase in number of children, the percentage of respondents also increases, thus showing no dependence of the two variables. Chi square test doesnot supports the finding of the empirical data in case of the 1990 data, showing dependence, while the 2002 data also does not go with chi-square results as it shows high dependence.

Management of family affairs if not working when seen with reference to age group children of the respondents, shows that as the **age group of children increases, the percent of women responding with would have been better managed, also decreases.** This trend is more pronounced in 1990.

When **no effect was reported with increase in age group of children, the percentage of women also increases,** again in 1990. In 2002, women with children of 14 years and above do not fall in tune with this trend. Application of X^2 test on 1990 data shows dependence, while the 2002 data shows no dependence of the two variables, which agrees with emperical findings.

Children are the most affected members of the family when the women go out for work. When respondents were asked to comment on the **reaction of their children to their going out for work, a majority of women say that their children have became used to her going out for work** (67.07% in 1990, and 65.15 % in 2002). Social workers are the chart toppers in both the studies (80.65 % in 1990, and 100.00% in the 2002 study).

When women report that their **children miss their presence** (20.12 % in the 1990 study, and 24.24% in the 2002 study), **maximum percent come from the profession of engineering** (43.48) **and medicine** (25.64) **in 1990, while doctors and nurses** (50.00 each) **say this in highest percentages in 2002.**

Medicine, nursing and engineering make heavy demands upon the time of the professional. To gain proficiency as well as do justice to these professions, a person must devote a great deal of time, away from home and children, to these exacting duties.

Irrespective of the family they come from, a majority of respondents report that their children have adjusted to the situation - joint family (60.00 and 53.17), and nuclear family (73.62 and 69.23). The percent of women reporting that their children miss them has increased in 2002, hailing from both the types of families (32.14 from joint family, 20.51 from nuclear family). In 1990 only 25.00% from joint family, and 15.30 % nuclear family reported of this incidence.

Clearly, **more working women professionals in 2002, report their children miss them when they go out for work, whether they hail from joint family or nuclear family.**

When the reaction of the children is seen with reference to period of service she has put in, the data **show that in both the studies, all the respondents who have just started their professional pursuit say their children miss them** (100.00% in 1990, as well as in 2002).

The assertion that their children have adjusted to the situation has been reported by all categories of women, in majority, irrespective of the number of years put in. No clear trend emerges from the data in both the studies.

On studing the **attitudes and beliefs of the working professionals,** when the respondents were asked to project their views on conflicts faced when the woman has just joined her profession, or when she has already spent a considerable number of years in her profession, **both the studies have professionals reporting that the longer the duration of service, lesser the conflicts** (73.90 and 55.83). The percent has come down in 2002, while respondents reporting no effect of time period has gone up in 2002 (10.66 in 1990, and 34.16 in 2002).

Here it may be inferred that there are factors other than time period devoted in profession, which are related to generation of conflict among working female professionals.

The professionals were asked whether it is easy to work at a stretch for the entire duration of working hours, or is it more convenient when the working hours are split into two or more time duties, as in case of doctors and lawyers (where they go for work in the morning, and then in the evening). **Majority of women said that conflict are more in many time duty** (77.55 and 63.33) **as it needs adjustment to be made again and again both by the family and by the professional herself. It also leads to loss of time in commuting and increases expenditure for the same.**

The suitability for a professionally qualified woman with respect to private practice, where the professionals set their own rules of working, when contrasted with employment where she is provided with the infrastructure to work but is limited by the norms and rules of the organisation, elicited the following response.

Practicing on their own is more risky and generates more role conflict according to women in both the studies (44.85% and 38.33%), which is a majority view in both the studies. But a sizeable percentage (23.90% in 1990, and 37.50% in 2002) also said that conflict is equal in both employment and in private practice, as both the situations have their inherent problems.

Conflict faced by the woman who is the sole earning member of the family, will be more, aver professionals in both the studies (77.57% in 1990, and 100.00% in 2002).

In both the studies, the respondents were of the opinion that professionally qualified women should also get married (80.52% in 1990, and 86.66% in 2002), for companionship and fulfillment in life. Only 4.41% women in 1990 were of the view that working professionals should not marry.

Optimum number of working hours for unmarried professionals has been pegged at **8 hours,** by the largest percent of respondents **in 1990,** while in **2002,** respondents were of the view that **unmarried female professionals can work for more than 8 hours,** without disturbing their expected life style. **Married women without children can also work for 8 hours per day,** according to 44.12 % in 1990, and 36.36 % in 2002. **Married women with children should ideally work for only 4-5 hours a day,** is the consensus of 64.34 % in 1990, which rose to 81.15 % in the 2002 study.

As far as the **image she elicits in the mind of other people,** about her professional status, is concerned, a large percent in both the studies (71.37 and 83.33) are of the opinion that **they assess a good image of themselves,** when interacting with people at large. Professionals from medicine (77.78 and 100.00), law (81.82 and 90.00), engineering (76.00 and 100.00), and teaching (82.98 and 100.00) said this in large percentages.

In the 2002 data, none of the professionals report of leaving a bad image in the minds of other people about their professional status. But in 1990, 5.99% of the respondents had the view that their working status generates a negative image in other people – nursing (16.00), engineering (8.00), social work (2.50), and teaching (2.13) were at the receiving end of this negative animus.

The reaction to the question whether professionally qualified women should take a plunge into their profession, on the basis of their professional (qualification) attainments or should they do so in certain circumstances: **in 1990, 68.75 % of the respondents were of the view that such women should adopt the profession if normal circumstances prevail** – law (81.82), engineering (78.00), and nursing (76.00).

In 2002 study, women are more assertive of their qualifications and professional status, and respond in large percentages (74.16), **that a professionally qualified women should pursue a career, under all circumstances.** It is also observed that the more high–profile the profession, higher is the percentage of respondents from the profession conforming to this view - engineering (100.00), medicine (80.00), law (90.00), while being a low-profile job, teaching commands only 50.00% approbation, for this view.

When asked about the **most suitable profession for females, both the studies have women voting for teaching profession** (88.01 and 42.50). It is best-suited profession for women because it is less demanding on time every day, and also has the added advantage of having vacations at the same time as their children do.

But the percent of women who **support** that **teaching** is the most suitable profession for a female has **considerably reduced in 2002,** giving way to other options like **dependence on the choice of the individual** (13.60 in the 1990 study, and 28.33 in the 2002 study).

Clearly, the women of today are ready to come out of the traditional mould, and pursue their academic, professional, creative, and even adventure related career options, with gusto hitherto encouraged in and displayed by the male child alone.

When confronted with after being in the profession for a considerable period of time what do they feel about their own profession, and how best is it suited to the contemporary women folk – **both the studies have women reporting no difference between the male and female competencies, as for as practicing the profession are concerned** (56.62 and 50.00). As has been the norm thus far, in both the studies, women professionals from medicine and engineering (76.00 each), voice this in the largest percentage in 1990, and in 2002, it is the doctors (75.00), and social workers (70.00) who give firm support to this assertion.

Their profession is more suitable for girls and women – overall 33.82% **in the 1990 study, and** 33.33 % **in the 2002 study, and profession wise, advocated by teachers** (56.00 and 70.00), **and nurses** (50.00 and 50.00). Females are **less suitable** for their profession – engineers (45.00), lawyers (25.00) in 2002, and in 1990 lawyers (25.00), and engineers (12.00). **Thus law and engineering are two professions found to be less suitable for women to pursue in both the studies.**

Qualities which a professionally qualified woman should ideally possess so as to reduce role conflict–both studies have respondents suggesting that the working women to **be compromising, adjusting and practical in her outlook** (30.15 and 30.83), **being active, swift** (27.21 and 29.16), **behaviour of women must be polite, humble and patient** (29.41 and 45.83).

Is a woman capable of doing all kinds of jobs, which a man does – aye (63.23 and 66.66). **Jobs not suitable for women, in view of the remaining respondents comprises up of jobs requiring excessive physical labour, touring, indefinite working hours.**

Trend among girls to opt for the profession they are in–women professionals in both the studies, from **medicine** (62.00 and 80.00) **and engineering** (64.00 and 100.00) say in the highest percentages, **that girls are happiest in joining their profession. Law** (5.00 in 2002) **and social work** (12.00 in 1990) **is studied when other alternatives are closed upon the girls.**

Discriminatory social altitude towards working women in the society at large – a majority of women in both the studies felt it is unjust (86.76 and 69.16). 16.66 % respondents in 2002 say it is non-existent now. None in 2002 was of the view that it is just. In 1990, 4.78 % respondents supported the view, and held that it is the attitude and behaviour of some working women who pass such signals which make people discriminate them, or show less acceptance toward working women.

Whether not allowing a qualified woman professional to take up professional practice is a violation of her human rights – 77.00 % women said aye in 2002, **it is undoubtedly a matter of violation of human rights.** But, 7.50% respondents also said that it depends upon the circumstances in which the professional is placed. If circumstances are against her taking up a job, then it is not a violation of her human rights. Only the respondents of 2002 study were subjected to this question, as in 1990, human rights issues were not so much in the forefront.

Many studies conducted in India, and abroad, also report of women facing discriminatory social attitude. But, Tara Ali Baig is of the view that Asian and African women are subjected to discrimination in lesser extent than their European and American counterparts.

The findings of the present study goes in coherence with the views of Ramu (1989) that in the last 5-6 decades, general factors eg. educational, economic and legal have coalesced, enabling women in particular of the urban middle and upper classes, to enter into the labour force. This has been seen by sociologists as a begining of a change in the status of women in marital and family structure.

CHAPTER 10

SUGGESTIONS FOR PREVENTING AND MINIMIZING ROLE CONFLICT

Suggestions for improvement in the condition of working women professionals by resolving the problem of role conflict faced while performing dual roles both at home and at the place of work can be classified into two broad categories

1. Suggestions given by the respondents
2. Recommendations made by the researcher

Suggestions given by the respondents

This section has been divided into 3 parts

i) Common suggestions given by the professionals in both the studies of 1990 and 2002

ii) Suggestions offered only in 1990 study

iii) Suggestions offered only in 2002 study

This segregation has been done to make explicit the change in contents of the suggestions in both the studies.

Common suggestion of both the studies

Only two common suggestions emerge in the two studies.

The first being **cooperation from people at home** - this is professed by professionals in largest majority (83.09% in 1990 and 61.66% in 2002 study). The percent in 2002 has reduced in comparison to 1990 but no other suggestion comes even close to this percentage thereby reflecting on the importance given to this factor by the professionals.

Profession wise break up runs as: Medicine (74.00 and 80.00), Law (90.91 and 50.00), Engineering (86.00 and 50.00), Teaching (84.00 and 75.00), Nursing (84.00 and 80.00), Social Work (84.00 and 60.00).

It can be observed from the above statistics that women from the professions of law, engineering, and social work have shown less concern for getting cooperation from their family members in performance of their dual responsibilities.

The other common suggestion is **cooperation from the people at the place of work.** (13.97% in 1990, and 22.50% in the 2002 study) Interestingly the percentage of professionals opining cooperation at the place of work has increased in the second study. This reflects the concern of the women to keep the conflict in check from the professional front.

The profession wise break up which stands as Medicine (18.00 and 20.00), Law (9.09 of 10.00), Engineering . (6.00 and 15.00) Teaching (16.00 and 20.00), Nursing (12.00 ad 30.00) and Social Work (20.00 and 40.00).

Percentages in most of the professions are close in both the studies except in case of nursing and social work where the percentages have shown considerable increase. Thus nurses and social workers are among those professionals who look forward to getting more cooperation from people at the place of work in today time.

People at the place of work refer to people higher up in the hierarchy, colleagues and subordinate and helping staff.

Suggestions obtained in 1990 study

The other suggestion given in little large percentage is joint family for the working professional (25.00). Another section of women (12.50), advocates joint family if the family accepts the working status of the woman. Reasons in support are that joint family will act as an anchor for the working professional and take over some of the responsibilities to be shouldered by her.

Professional to be good natured and compromising in their attitude, was professed by some of the respondents (20.59). They shouldn't be adamant about their stance and generally remain good natured so as not to vitiate the environment, or add to the tense environment.

Another 9.19 % respondents were of the opinion that the working professional should be proficient in work management as she has double the load of work. If management of work is sloppy, she will not be able to be abreast with of the requirements attached to both the responsibilities.

Some of the other pragmatic and practical suggestions were also put forth by respondents individually from different professions

1 Woman should be clear and specific about their goals when going out for work (Social Work)

2 Woman should take up only those professions which suit their temperament (Social Work)

3 Women should choose a partner with equal mental maturity (Social Work and Teaching)

4 Women should have confidence in their abilities. (Teaching and Medicine)

5 Working professional should contribute to family expenditure to gain acceptance by the family members (Teaching)

6 Women in profession should understand the psychology of people around them (Teaching)

7 Working women should cultivate some hobby to underline tension (Medicine).

Suggestions obtained in 2002 study

Suggestions which the respondents gave in the later study were more diversified and pragmatic. Some of the respondents came out with

Table : 10.1 : Suggestions offered by respondents to reduce role conflict among working women professional in 1990

Suggestions	Type of profession						
	Medicine	**Law**	**Engineering**	**Teaching**	**Nursing**	**Social Work**	**Total**
Joint Family	14.00	45.45	22.22	10.00	24.00	46.00	25.00
Nuclear Family	-	18.18	10.00	4.00	-	-	4.04
Appreciation of work both at home and the place of work	16.00			8.00	48.00	8.00	6.25
Human Consideration with regards to work load and time, at the place of work	-	-	-	4.00	8.00	-	2.20
Work management by the professional	12.00	27.27	4.00	10.00	10.00	2.00	9.19
Professional should be good natured and compromising	14.00	27.27	26.00	18.00	16.00	26.00	20.59

Maintain a balance between work at home and at the place of work	2.00	-	2.00	8.00	-	4.00	2.94
If people at home accept the working woman, then joint family is ideal	10.00	27.27	20.00	4.00	4.00	18.00	12.50
Creating awareness through education especially of women folk	14.00	9.09	-	8.000	8.00	-	6.25
Good working conditions	10.00	-	2.00	2.00	-	-	2.57
Working woman should not be touchy	4.00	-	-	6.00	-	-	1.84
Women should maintain dignity and respect	-	-	2.00	2.00	2.00	-	1.10
Small family	2.00	-	2.00	2.00	-	-	1.10
Working woman should not be egotistic	12.00		4.00	4.00		6.00	4.78
Base	**100.00**	**100.00**	**100.00**	**100.00**	**100.00**	**100.00**	**100.00**

very novel and unconventional suggestions, so that the woman is able to do justice to both of her roles (at home and the place of work). In this section, suggestions offered in sizeable percents have been given in tabular form followed by suggestion given by respondents in a small numbers and even by individual respondents.

Table : 10.2 : Suggestions offered by respondents to reduce role conflict among working women professionals in 2002

Suggestions	Type of profession						
	Medicine	Law	Engineering	Teaching	Nursing	Social Work	Total
Right attitude on the part of the professional	60.00	35.00	40.00	30.00	30.00	20.00	19.16
Self dependent	-	-	10.00	-	10.00	-	3.32
Good communication amongst the family members	10.00		35.00	-	10.00	10.00	10.83
Creche facility	-	-	20.00	-	10.00	-	5.00
Conveyance facility	-	15.00	-	-	10.00	-	4.16
Spouse and in-laws to to have positive attitude towards her working	10.00	20.00	-	10.00	10.00	20.00	11.66
Flexible timing	-	-	-	20.00	-	-	3.32
Helping hand in the form of maid	10.00	-	10.00	10.00	10.00	15.00	9.16
Media image of women should be positive	10.00	10.00	50.00	10.00	5.00	20.00	17.5
Change in work Culture and social system	-	15.00	15.00		-	10.00	6.66
Part time jobs for women	-	10.00	15.00	10.00	-	-	5.83
Base	100.00	100.00	100.00	100.00	100.00	100.00	100.00

Here 19.16% of the professionals are of the view that the right attitude on the part of the working women will lead to minimum conflicts in performing the balancing act. Right attitude here refers to the women being not very sentimental about trivial issues, or being egoistic about her stance. But she should have a voice of her own where she can explain her perspective to people in a cool and calm way.

Self-dependency is advocated by 3.32% respondents. Self dependency relates to those kinds of work which may not come under her direct roles but affect her functioning eg. going to the bank or going for the parent-teacher meeting of her children. Rather than waiting for somebody to help her she should be self dependent in managing such jobs on her own.

10.83% respondents were of the opinion that open communication channels amongst the family members will lead to better understanding of each others role expectations and level of role performance.

Availability of creche at the place of work will make working easier for women, opined 5.00% of the respondents. 4.16% professionals were of the view that availability of conveyance for the professional will reduce the time and stress of commuting, thereby reducing conflicts.

Another 11.66% professionals were of the opinion that if the attitude of the spouse (husband) and in-law is positive towards the working status of the woman, the conflicts get reduced as they will have less expectation from her on the home front. They will realise her dual role play and they will lend a helping hand to her in taking care of her domestic responsibilities.

The concept of flexi-timings is gaining momentum in Indian cities in today's time. This has been of the view of 3.32% of the respondents, that this concept will help in taking care dual of responsibilities in a more stress and conflict free manner.

Extra helping-hand in the form of a maid does help in catering to the domestic responsibilities of the professionals by proving a respite for them, thus helping in reducing the potential of conflict.

Respondents in small percentage (6.60) advocate change in culture and social systems which will also lead to reducing conflicts for the working women. Change in culture means shedding such stereotypes that challenging jobs shouldn't be handled by women. They are generally given the routine monotonous, jobs basically to under play the capabilities of women professionals. Change in the social systems relates to the fact that women should be amalgamated with in all the social system like economic, political and religious, in more amiable manner, rather than women forcing themselves in through agitations – change must be natural and become part of every social system.

Part time jobs have also been suggested by 5.83% professional but Ranade and Ram Chandran's study (1970) found that women show less preference towards part-time jobs than to full time employment. In the present context, the professionals being from specialized fields may make reasonable economic gains from part-time employment and have the satisfaction of remaining in touch with the profession. Once the children grow up she can always revert to full time engagement in her profession.

Secondly the avenues for professional pursuit are also more in the sense that the professional may go for employed status or private practice of the profession (in which case she can have more liberty and flexibility with respect to the time devoted for the profession).

A sizeable percent of professionals (17.50) aver that a positive image of the working women should be projected by the media rather than showing women as high handed, irresponsible, of loose character and not adhering to family values. These kind of malicious projections lead to erroneous impression about the character of the working women in the eye of the common people.

Some suggestion offered by individuals or by a small group of respondents.

(a) Doctors

- Create more awareness in the society
- Prepare boys from childhood to have a positive outlook towards working women
- The professional should be self-contained and not over ambitious.

(b) Lawyers

- Elevate educational status of the women
- Orthodox views should be disowned by people

- Working professional should be encouraged to show good results.

(c) **Engineers**

- Optimal resources utilization (both internal and external)
- Concentrate more on your expertise rather than trying to be jack of all trades.
- A working professional should be less conscious about societal views
- Professionals if raising her family should be allowed to take readmission into technical courses after the age of 35 years, when they have raised their family, to put herself abreast of the latest development and then plunge into the professional pursuit with recouped vigour.
- Selection of the partner should be judicious so as to avoid conflict on the account of taking up of professional practice.

d) **Teachers**

- She should be bold and reserve.
- She should not spend extra-time out after the job gets over. (should not loiter after working hours)

(e) **Social Workers**

- If the nature of the job allows, the professional must be given a choice of operation from home, as well.
- There should be less expectations with regards to socialization from her.

Recommendations made by the researcher.

The problem of role conflict arise mainly because of an ambivalent situation in which the house hold role, occupational role and position in the society (societal status) are not evenly balanced. Hence, it becomes necessary to end this ambivalence and appropriate measures be taken at different level, viz (1) at the level of Individual working woman (2) at the level of the family (3) at the level of the employer or work level (4) and lastly, at the level of society at large.

(1) ***Measures to be taken at the level of individual woman.***

The working female professional will have to bring about the following changes in her personality and orientation so as to combat the problem of role conflict.

(a) She should develop a realistic and pragmatic behaviour in her day to day life. She has not to become emotional and make a prestige issue for every small event in her daily chores/duties both at home and the place of work.

(b) She should gain acceptance of her new role from family members, neighbours and people in her community through her behaviour which may vary according to the requirement of the situation, between the two extremes co-operation and gentle behaviour to confronting any changes to be brought about in the mind set of people.

(c) The working female has to be highly systematic and shall have to develop managerial skills.

(d) The working professional will have to remain in good heath to take up her dual responsibilities. Ill health may make her look for excuses for not being able to cope up with work pressure and thus add to her problems or even create new ones for her.

(2) **Measures to be taken at the level of family**

It is necessary that members of the family develop a co-operative attitude towards these working female professionals in the family. They should try to realise the problems, difficulties and also the feelings of the professional.

They should also adopt a helping altitude, share her burden of work and make their best possible endeavour to make the environment happy at home. If motivation and appreciation is added to this, female professional can scale new heights and bring name and fame to her family

3) **Measure to be taken at work place**

The people at work place, especially the higher ups, will have to change their attitude towards working women by accepting the reality that they, are equally competent, as men in undertaking all kinds of jobs. Female professionals should be considered as assets and not liabilities and should not be dumped in a corner as worthless.

On the other hand they should be encouraged to take up the more innovative and challenging part of their professional pursuits, so that their best talents and potentials may be tapped and used for the good of the nation at large. Employers should shun all kind of tendencies to exploit the female professional on account of her gender.

Their male colleagues will also have to change their attitude and behaviour by accepting the working women as their equal and shed their tendency of putting them in a trap situation in order to exploit them.

The last but not the least an organization or employer in consideration of the added responsibilities of working female professionals at home front also, should consider bringing in the concept of flexible timings for them. This will not only reduce their role-conflicts but also increase their efficiency upon both fronts.

An extract from Business India (September 1991), substantiates the point in consideration- for most people who arrive at work exhausted by peak hour traffic or early morning domestic crisis, the freedom to choose ones working hours must seem like a distant dream. Yet, the concept of flexible timing has been gaining credence world wide. The trend is slowly catching up in India also. Bayer's Deputy Manager (Training) Ritu Singhal is of the opinion that (flexible timing) is very advantageous to women who are sadled with house hold chores. Bayer has found that absenteeism has dropped since the introduction of flexible timings.

Jerry D'Souza, Manager (HRD), Herbertsons, points out – Flexible timings meet individuals requirements without being disadvantageous to the organization. It helps efficiency because every one does not have to adjust to fixed timings.

But, Lerner (1994), has reflected in her study that sometimes the best choice for a women who desires to combine employment and family is to work part time especially when her children are young and alternative care is expensive . Part time or flexible employment however is neither available nor advantageous to all.

Measures to be taken at the level of society

Chanana (2000) is of the view that if women have to contribute as full members of the society, their potential must be harnessed especially when they have demonstrated their capacity to succeed in educational systems.

There has been a general change in societal attitudes and values, particularly in the area of giving equal importance to occupational work by women.

There should be reservation of jobs for needful women; take war widows, women whose husband die in factory accidents etc. Secondly, there should be enforcement of legal provision and strict penalty, to deal with those who infringe the rights of women, particularly those who exploit working woman by taking undue advantage of their vulnerable employment situation.

Devendra Kiran (1985) is of the view that as women are vulnerable group with fewer opportunities, they have been affected more adversely than men (urbanization and globalization). Whether this situation improves or is aggrevated further depends upon thee level and extent of the infrastructure provided. This will include education, vocational and technical training, special measures to adjust women's employment to their special needs as house wife, mother and to prevent discrimination and exploitation.

Public opinion should be moulded for working women that day can look after their families better when they fulfil their duties at home and at work place simultaneously. And for this, they surely need encouragement especially from their family.

To conclude, it can be said that a comprehensive movement has to be launched and activated to transform the negative attitude, towards working women professionals right from the stage of childhood. Such an enterprise can succeed only with the stringent enforcement of law, social commitment and political will.

BIBLIOGRAPHY

1. Agarwal, K.G. (1978) : Self Role and Status, Sterling Publishers Pvt Ltd, New Delhi.
2. Agnew, Vijal (1986) : Elite Women in Indian Politics, Vikas Publishing House, Delhi.
3. Anderson, N. (1961) : Work and Leisure, Routledge and Kegan Paul, London.
4. Arya, Sadhna (2000) : Women, Gender, Equality and the state, Deep and Deep Publications Pvt. Ltd, Delhi.
5. Baig, Tara Ali (1958): Women of India, Publications Division, Government of India, New Delhi.
6. Bajpai (1966) : Methods of Social Survey Research, Kitab Mahal, Kanpur.
7. Bhai, Nirmala P. (1986) : Harijan Women in Independent India, B.R. Publishing Corporation, Delhi.
8. Blood, Robert and Wolf Donald (1960) : Husbands and Wives The Dynamics of Married Living, Free Press, New York.
9. Bogardus, Emory, (1961) : Sociology, Mac Millan and Co., New York.
10. Carson, William, F., (1915) : The Marriage Revolt, Warner Lawice Ltd, London.
11. Chakraborty, Krishna (1983) : Conflicting Worlds of Working Mothers. A Sociological Enquiry.
12. Chaurasia, B.P. (1992) : Women's Status in India (Policies and Programmes) Chugh Publications, Allahabad.
13. Chawhan, Indira (1986) : Purdaah to Profession, B.R. Publishing Corporation, Delhi.

14. Cormac, Margaret (1961) : The Hindu Woman, Asia Publishing House, Delhi.
15. Davis, Kingsley (1961) : Human Society, Mac Millan Co., New York.
16. Das, R.M. (1962) : Women in Manu and His Seven Commentators, Kanchan Publications, Varanasi.
17. Debamout, Sara (1980) : The Sociology of Women : An Introduction, George Allen and Unwin, London.
18. Desai, N. (1957) : Women in Modern India, Vora and Co., Bombay.
19. Desai, Neera, Patel Vibhuti (1985) : Indian Women Change and Challenges in the International Decade 1975-85, Popular Prakashan, Bombay.
20. Devendra, Kiran (1985) : Status and Position of Woman in India, Vikas Publishing House, Ghaziabad.
21. Devi, K. Uma (2000) : Women, Gender, Equality and the State, Deep and Deep Publications Pvt. Ltd. Delhi.
22. Devi, V. Zalith (1982) : Status and Employment of Women in India, B. R. Publishing Corporation, Delhi.
23. Doranne, Jacobson, Susan and S Wadley (1977) : Women in India, Manohar Book Service.
24. Dube, S.C. (1973) : Men's and Women's Roles in India : A Sociological Review, in Barbara, (ed.), Women in New Asia, Paris : UNESCO.
25. Elliot, Merill (1976) : Social Disorganisation, Harper Brother, New York.
26. Gadgil (1961) : Women in the Working Force in India, Asia Publishing House, Bombay.
27. Gandhi, M.K. (1958) : Women and Social Injustice, Navjiwan Publishing House, Ahmedabad.
28. Garskof (M) Ed (1971) : Roles Women Play Reading Towards Women's Liberalization, Wadsworth Publishing Co. California.
29. Gertrude, Williams (1945) : Women at work, Nicholson and Watson, London.
30. Ghosh, S.K. (1984) : Women in a Changing Society, Asish Publishing House, New Delhi.

31. Ginsberg, Berg, Brown, Carol (1967) : Life Style of Educated Women, Columbia University Press, New Delhi.

32. Gore, M.S. (1968) : Urbanisation and Family Change, Popular Prakashan, Bombay.

33. Grace, R. Gerald (1972) : Conflicts and the Teacher, Routledge and Kegan Paul, London.

34. Green, Earnest (1978) : Personal Relations : An Approach to Marriage and Family, Mc Graw Hill Co.,

35. Gulati, J.S. (1956) : Careers for Women, YMCA Publishing House, New Delhi.

36. Gulati, Saroj (1985) : Women and Society, Chanakya Publications, Delhi.

37. Hate, A. Chandra Kala (1969) : Changing Status of Women : In Post Independence India, Allied Publislers Pvt Ltd, Delhi.

38. Her Highness of Baroda, Mitra S.M. (1981) : The Position of Women in Indian Life, Neeraj Publishing House, New Delhi.

39. Jha, K.N. (1985) : Women Towards Modernization, Chauhhata, Patna.

40. Johnson, H.M. (1966) : Sociology : A Systematic Introduction, Allied Publishers, Bombay.

41. Lerner Jacqualine V. (1994) : Working women and their families, family studies, Text series 13, Sage Publication, Thousand Oaks, London and New Delhi.

42. Kachroo, J.L. (1981) : General Sociology, Book Hive Publication, Delhi.

43. Kala, Rani (1976) : Role Conflict of Working Women, Chetna, New Delhi.

44. Kalbagh (ed.). (1992) : Women in enterprise and profession, Discovery Publication House, New Delhi.

45 Kapadia, K.M. (1968) : Marriage and Family in India, Oxford University Press, New Delhi.

46. Kapoor, Promila (1970) : Marriage and the Working Women in India, Vikas Publishing House, New Delhi.

47. __________, (1975) : The Changing Role and Status of Women, in the Indian Family in the Change and Challenges of the Seventies, (ISI Publications), Sterling Publishers Pvt Ltd, New Delhi.

48. ________, (1987) : The Changing Status of Working Women in India, Vikas Publishing House, New Delhi.

49. Klein, Viola (1946) : The Feminine Character , Kegan Paul, Trench Trubner and Co Ltd, New York.

50. ________, (1965) : Britians Married Women Workers, Rout ledge and Kegan Paul, New York.

51. Klein, Myrdal (1970) : Women' Two Roles : Home and Work, Routledge and Kegan Paul, London.

52. Krech David, Crutchfield RS, and Ballachey : Individual in Society, McGraw Hill Books Co., New York 1962.

53. Krishna, Kumari N.S. (1987) : Status of Single Woman in India, Uppal Publishing House, New Delhi.

54. Kumar, Hajra (ed.) (2000) : Status of Muslim women in India, Aakas Books, New Delhi.

55. Lewis (1965) : A. Coser, Bernard Rosenberg : Sociological Theory, The Mac Millan Company, New York.

56. Mal, Bhadur (1955) : Mental Health in Theory and Practice, Visheesh Varhath Research Institute, Hoshiarpur.

57. Mamoria, C.B. (1981) : Social Problems and Social Disorganization in India, Kitab Mahal, Allahabad.

58. Mehta, Rama (1975) : Divorced Hindu Women, Delhi : Vikas Publishing House, New Delhi.

59. Merill, Elliot (1976) : Social Disorganisation, Harper and Brother, New York.

60. Merton, L. Robert (1968) : Social Theory and Social Structure, Amerind Publishing Co Pvt. Ltd, New York.

61. Montagu, Ashley (1954) : Natural Superiority of Women, George Allen and Unwin Ltd, London.

62. Morris, Peter (1958) : Widows and Their Families, Routledge and Kegan Paul, London.

63. Mukherji, Radha Kamal (1957) : The Horizon of Marriage, Asia Publishing House, Bombay.

64. Munn, L. Norman (1961) : The Fundamentals of Human Adjustment, George G. Harrap and Co Ltd, London.

65. Musgrave Beatrice (1972) : Women at work, Peter Owen Ltd., London.

66. Nanda, B.R. (1976) : Indian Women : From Purdaah to Modernity, Vikas Publishing House, New Delhi.

67. Nadel S F (1969) : The Theory of Social Culture, Routledge and Kegan Paul, London.

68. Nimkoff Ogburin (1972) : Hand Book of Sociology, Eurasaia Publishing House (Pvt) Ltd, New Delhi.

69. Page, Maciver (1967) : Society in Introductory Analysis, Maconittan and Company Ltd, London.

70. Pal, B.K. (ed.) (1987) : Problems and Concern of Indian Women, ABC Publication, New Delhi.

71. Parker, Anderson (1966) : Society, Affiliated East West Press Pvt Ltd, New Delhi.

72. Persell, Hodges Caroline (1987) : Understanding Sociology, Harper and Row Publishers Inc., London.

73. Prabhu, P.H. (1963) : Hindu Social Organization, Popular Book Depot, Bombay.

74. Raghvan, Veera; Singh, Shalini and Khandelwal, Kanika (ed.) 2002: The Child in New Millenium, Mosai Books, New Delhi.

75. Rao, Anant and Kapoor (1986) : Women at work in India : A Bibliography, Sage Publication, New Delhi.

76. Usha, Rao, J.J. (1985) : Women In a Developing Society, Ashish Publishing House, New Delhi.

77. Ralph, R. (1976) : Roles and Relationships, Routledge and Kegan Paul, London.

78. Ramu, G. N. (1989) : Women, Work and Marriage in Urban India, Sage Publication, New Delhi/New Bury Park, London.

79. Rani, Kala (1976) : Role Conflict in Working Women, Chetan Publications, New Delhi.

80. Ray, Renuka (ed.) (1978) : Role and Status of Women in Indian Society, FIRMA, KLM Pvt. Ltd. Calcutta.

81. Reddy, C.R. (1986) : Chasnging Status of Educated Working Women, B.R. Publishing Corporation, Delhi.

82. ________, (1987) : Research Methodology in Social Sciences, Daya Publishing House, Delhi.

83. Richardson, D. and Robinson, V. (ed.) (1993) : Introducing Women's Studies, The Macmillan Press Ltd., London.

84. Ruddock, Ralph (1976) : Roles and Relationships, Routledge and Kegan Paul, London.

85. Sachidanand and Sinha, R.P. Ramesh (1984) : Women's Right : Myth and Reality, Printwell Publishers, Jaipur.

86. Sachaefer, T. Richard (1986) Sociology, Mc Graw Hill Book Company, London.

87. Sengupta, Padmini (1960) : Women Workers of India, Asia Publishing House, Delhi.

88. Sharma, A. N. and Sujit S. (ed.) (1993) : Women and Work: Changing Scenario in India B. R. Publishing, Delhi.

89. Singh, P.P. (1991) : Women in India : A Statistic Panorama, ABC Publcations, New Delhi.

90. Singh, Surendra and Srivastava, O.P. (2001) : Gender, Equality Through Women's Empowerment, Bharat Book Centre, Lucknow.

91. Singh, Y.A. (1977) : Modernization of Indian Tradition, Thompson Press Ltd, New Delhi.

92. Sood, Rita (1991) : Changing Status and Adjustment of Women, Manak Publications, Pvt. Ltd. Jaipur/Delhi.

93. Srivastava, A.K. (1986) : Social Class and Family Life in India, Chugh Publications, Allahabad.

94. Subamma, Malladi (1986) : Women Tradition and Culture, Sterling Publications, New Delhi.

95. Sutherland and Robert (1966) : Introductory Sociology, Oxford and IBH Publication Co., Calcutta.

96. Swarjya, Laxmi C. (1992) : Women at Work: Insights from Indian Organizations, Discovery Publishing House, New Delhi.

97. Swarukar, G.P. (1986) : Women Participation in Rural Environment, Chugh Publication, Allahabad.

98. Talwar, Usha (1984) : Social Profile of Working Women, Jam Brothers, Jodhpur.

99. Tanwar Reicha (ed.) (1998): Women: Human Rights, Religion and Violence, Nirmal Book Agency, Kurukshetra.

100. Thomas. P. (1939) : Women and Marriage in India, George Allen and Unwin Ltd, London.

101. Wadley, Dronne; Jacobson, Susaris (1977) : Women in India, Manohar Book Service, New Delhi.

102. Ward, Barbara (ed.) (1973) : Women in the New Asia, Paris UNESCO.

103. Wesner and Denmark (ed.) (1976) : Women Vol. I, APDI Reserch Reference Work, Psychological Dimensions INC, New York.

104. Wood Ward, Maxwell, Sutherland (1966) : Introductory Sociology (Sixth ed.), Oxford and IBH Publishing Go, Delhi.

105. Young, P.V. (1961) : Scientific Social Surveys and Research, Asia Publishing House, Bombay.

106. Young, Kimball (1972) : Systematic Sociology, Affliate East West Press Pvt Ltd, New Delhi.

Dictionary, Encyclopaedia, Journals, Dissertations, Abstracts, Reports, Unpublished Thesis. etc.

1. Bhatia, Pratima (1976) : Role Conflict Among Working Women, Unpublished Ph.D. Thesis of Lucknow University.

2. Blackwell (2000) : Dictionary of Sociology.

3. Dhingra, O. P. (1972) : Women in Employment "A Report, Sri Ram Centre for Industriall Relation and Human Resources, New Delhi.

4. Esther, Robinson (1978) : Strain and Dual Occupation Among Women, Dissertation Abstract International, Vol.38, No.7, January.

5. Joseph, Sarah (1987) : Equality a Release from Oppression, Surya India, June.

6. Jauhri, Prema (1968) : Status of Working Women, Unpublished Ph.D. Thesis of Lucknow University.

7. Lexicon Universal Encyclopaedia, Vol.16, Lexicon Publications, New York.

8. Locke, Harvey and Mackesprang, Murid (1979) : Marital Adjustment of the Employed Wife, American Journal of Sociology, May.

9. London School of Economics (1960) : Women Wife and Worker, Department of Social Services, Published by Her Majesty's Stating Office.

10. Mahajan, A. (1966) : Women's two roles: A Study of Role Conflicts, the Indian Journal of Social Work, Vol. XXVI.

11. Mitchell, Duncan (ed.) (1968) : The Dictionary of Sociology, Routledge and Kegan Paul, London.

12. Penguin Dictionary of Sociology, (1986).

13. Penguin Dictionary of Psychology, (1986).

14. Ranade, S.N. and Ramachandran (1970) : Women and Employment, Tata Institute of Social Sciences, Bombay.

15. Rastogi, Shail Bala : Working Women in an Urban Setting, Unpublished Ph.D. Thesis of Lucknow University.

16. Rawat, Harikrishna (1986) : Encyclopaedia of Sociology (Concepts), Vol.1, Rawat Publications, Jaipur.

17. Saxena, Archana : Role Conflict Among Working Women Unpublished Ph.D. Thesis of Kanpur University.

18. Singh and Gupta (1978) : Impact of Serving Mothers on the Academic Attainent of Their Children, The Educational Trend, Vol.13, January.

19. The Dictionary of Family Psychology and Family Therapy (1993).

20. Von Mering, F.H. (1955) : Professional and Non–Professional Women as Mothers., Journal of Social Psychology, No.42, August.

21. William Goode, J . A. (1976) : Theory of Role Strain American Sociological Review, Vol. 25, No. 4.

INDEX

S

T

U

V